Contagious Christianity

A Study of 1 Thessalonians

BIBLE STUDY GUIDE

From the Bible-teaching ministry of

Charles R. Swindoll

INSIGHT FOR LIVING

Charles R. Swindoll is a graduate of Dallas Theological Seminary and has served as senior pastor of the First Evangelical Free Church of Fullerton, California, since 1971. Chuck's radio program, "Insight for Living," began in 1979. In addition to his church and radio ministries, Chuck enjoys writing. He has authored numerous books and booklets on a variety of subjects.

Based on the outlines and transcripts of Chuck's sermons, the study guide text is co-authored by Bryce Klabunde, a graduate of Biola University and Dallas Theological Seminary. He also wrote the Living Insights sections.

Editor in Chief:
Cynthia Swindoll

Coauthor of Text:
Bryce Klabunde

Assistant Editor:
Wendy Peterson

Copy Editors:
Deborah Gibbs
Cheryl Gilmore
Glenda Schlahta

Designer:
Gary Lett

Publishing System Specialist:
Bob Haskins

Director, Communications Division:
Deedee Snyder

Manager, Creative Services:
Alene Cooper

Project Supervisor:
Susan Nelson

Print Production Manager:
John Norton

Printer:
Sinclair Printing Company

Unless otherwise identified, all Scripture references are from the New American Standard Bible, © The Lockman Foundation 1960, 1962, 1963, 1968, 1971, 1972, 1973, 1975, 1977. Used by permission.

Scripture taken from the Holy Bible, New International Version, Copyright © 1973, 1978, 1984 International Bible Society, used by permission of Zondervan Bible Publishers.

The other translation cited is *The Message: The New Testament in Contemporary English* by Eugene H. Peterson, (Colorado Springs, Colo.: NavPress, 1993), p. 434.

An effort has been made to locate sources and obtain permission where necessary for the quotations used in this book. In the event of any unintentional omission, a modification will gladly be incorporated in future printings.

ISBN 0-8499-8481-5
Printed in the United States of America

COVER DESIGN: Nina Paris
COVER PHOTOGRAPH: The Stock Market

CONTENTS

INTRODUCTION

The first letter of Paul's to find its way into the collection of New Testament books was 1 Thessalonians. Although rather brief, it is one of the most positive and insightful statements we can read that portrays a first-century congregation. Those Thessalonians were downright contagious!

In our day, when the church is all too often viewed with jaded, cynical eyes, this affirming letter needs to be declared. I believe you will be encouraged and challenged as we work our way through it, verse by verse.

Ultimately, I hope this study will boost the morale of many whose Christianity has begun drifting dangerously close to mediocrity. I know of few things that are better able to halt this disease than a massive dose of 1 Thessalonians taken on a daily basis.

Chuck Swindoll

Chuck Swindoll

PUTTING TRUTH
INTO ACTION

Knowledge apart from application falls short of God's desire for His children. He wants us to apply what we learn so that we will change and grow. This study guide was prepared with these goals in mind. As you go through the following pages, we hope your desire to discover biblical truth will grow as your understanding of God's Word increases, and that you will be encouraged to apply what you've learned.

To assist you in your study, we've included a section called Living Insights at the end of each lesson. These exercises will challenge you to study further and to think of specific ways to put your discoveries into action.

There are many ways to use this guide—in personal devotions, group studies, discussions with friends and family, and Sunday school classes. And, of course, it's an ideal study aid when you're listening to its corresponding "Insight for Living" radio series.

To benefit most from this study guide, we would encourage you to consider it a spiritual journal. That's why we've included space in the Living Insights for recording your thoughts and discoveries. We hope you'll return to those sections often for review and encouragement as you continue to grow in your walk with Christ.

Bryce Klabunde
Coauthor of Text
Author of Living Insights

Contagious Christianity

A Study of I Thessalonians

Chapter 1

A CHURCH WITH THE RIGHT STUFF

1 Thessalonians 1

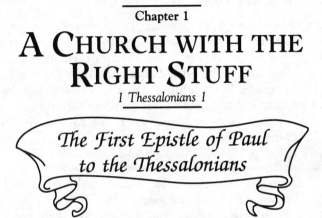

The First Epistle of Paul to the Thessalonians

I t's a rather daunting title, isn't it? Originally, though, it was just a heart-to-heart letter from a pastor, Paul, to a struggling young church in the Greek city of Thessalonica.

About a year had passed since a storm of persecution swept Paul away from the Thessalonians, leaving them as mere saplings in their faith. He had to wonder if they could weather the tumult alone. So much was at stake—these people, this city, the momentum of the Faith was on the line. According to commentator William Barclay,

> It is impossible to overstress the importance of the arrival of Christianity in Thessalonica. If Christianity was settled there, it was bound to spread East along the Egnatian Road until all Asia was conquered and West until it stormed even the city of Rome. The coming of Christianity to Thessalonica was crucial in the making of it into a world religion. . . .
>
> Thessalonica was a test case; and Paul was torn with anxiety to know how it would turn out.[1]

1. William Barclay, *The Letters to the Philippians, Colossians, and Thessalonians*, rev. ed., The Daily Study Bible Series (Philadelphia, Pa.: Westminster Press, 1975), p. 181.

Did the Thessalonian church have the "right stuff" to survive and grow? Through our study of Paul's letter, we'll discover the answer. And we'll discover what it takes to develop a stronger faith and greater joy in our own lives—the kind of Christianity that not only lasts but spreads. A *contagious* Christianity.

Realism: Key to a Balanced Perspective

Do you ever struggle with relating to the people in Scripture? Sometimes we tend to see them as bigger than life, never wrestling with doubt or shivering in fear like us. Dressing them in saintly white robes, we cloak their faith in idealism and think we could never have their courage. But truthfully, their halos were just as non-existent as ours. To balance our perspective and see these believers as they really were—young Christians trying to find their way—let's take an in-depth look at this very first church in Thessalonica.

The Founder

Paul had founded the church as he was traveling through Macedonia on his second missionary journey. According to Acts 17:2, he preached Christ in the synagogue for only "three Sabbaths."[2] In that short time, some Jews

> were persuaded and joined Paul and Silas, along with
> a great multitude of the God-fearing Greeks and a
> number of the leading women. (v. 4)

Paul must have been an eloquent speaker with a winsome personality to draw such an immediate response, right? Actually, he was just the opposite. According to some people in the Corinthian church,

> "his letters are weighty and strong, but his personal
> presence is unimpressive, and his speech contempt-
> ible."[3] (2 Cor. 10:10)

2. Paul could have been in Thessalonica longer than "three Sabbaths," or weeks—possibly as long as five weeks. He had to have time to work for his income (1 Thess. 2:9) and receive at least two financial gifts from the Philippian believers (Phil. 4:16). Even so, it is remarkable that he was able to start the church so quickly.

3. One ancient writer elaborated on Paul's "unimpressive" appearance: [He was] "a man of little stature, thin-haired upon the head, crooked in the legs, of good state of body, with eyebrows meeting, and with nose somewhat hooked." From *The Acts of Paul and Thecla*, as quoted by William Barclay in *The Letters to the Corinthians*, rev. ed., The Daily Study Bible Series (Philadelphia, Pa.: Westminster Press, 1975), pp. 242–43.

Paul was certainly no handsome, golden-throated evangelist. Yet God spoke through his weaknesses to reach many people in the bustling city of Thessalonica.

The City

Situated on the Via Egnatia, the city boasted a host of economic opportunities. According to William Barclay,

> its main street was part of the very road which linked Rome with the East. East and West converged on Thessalonica; it was said to be "in the lap of the Roman Empire." Trade poured into her from East and West, so that it was said, "So long as nature does not change, Thessalonica will remain wealthy and prosperous."[4]

It was also a free city in the Roman Empire—a prized status, one the authorities felt was being threatened when a raucous mob started making wild accusations against some of the new believers. And Christianity got the blame.

The Situation

Briefly, here's what happened. As the truth of the gospel won over more and more people, a group of jealous Jews along with "some wicked men from the market place" accused the young Christians of acting "contrary to the decrees of Caesar" (Acts 17:5–7). They put the whole city in an uproar and dragged some of the brethren out of a man's house to face the city leaders. It was a frightening episode, and as a result, Paul was forced to flee the city by night (v. 10).

After several agonizing months away, he "could endure it no longer" and sent Timothy to report on the believers' welfare (1 Thess. 3:1, 5). In response to Timothy's good word about them, he wrote them a letter from Corinth to *affirm* their steadfast faith, to *exhort* them to excel even more, and to *inform* them about what to expect in the future.[5]

---

4. Barclay, *The Letters to the Philippians, Colossians, and Thessalonians*, p. 180.

5. First Thessalonians was probably Paul's first letter, written about A.D. 50. However, some commentators believe Galatians came first, dating it around A.D. 48.

Balance: Secret of a Committed Congregation

This letter of Paul's has much to offer us. It is a beacon of light to guide us past rocky extremes of fanaticism or complacency. And like a lighthouse in a storm, it provides us comfort, hope, and direction. Let's watch for these flashes of light throughout the book as we study it verse by verse, beginning with Paul's opening lines, which overflow with gratitude toward the Lord.

Thanking

> Paul and Silvanus and Timothy to the church of the Thessalonians in God the Father and the Lord Jesus Christ: Grace to you and peace.
> We give thanks to God always for all of you, making mention of you in our prayers. (1 Thess. 1:1–2)

Paul writes on behalf of his two companions—Silvanus, also known as Silas, and Timothy, who had been with him in Thessalonica. Although he addresses his letter to the Thessalonian church, Paul's message applies just as much to the churches we attend. For, like them, we need to be open to the truth—receivers of God's spiritual signals rather than just broadcasters of our own brand of teaching.

Notice what else Paul says about this church: they were "in God the Father and the Lord Jesus Christ." That's our heavenly address too—in the Father *and* the Son. We are safe in the hands of Jesus, and Jesus is safe in the hands of the Father. That's double security!

Based on that promise, Paul wishes the Thessalonians a life of grace and peace. Christ's blood satisfied the wrath of God that once hung over us all like a dark cloud (1 John 2:1–2). However, now that we enjoy the sunshine of God's grace, we can live as God intended, free from guilt and filled with peace.

Paul also thanks God for the Thessalonians. He found it easy to remember to pray for them because they had won his heart with their sincere devotion to Christ.

How can we be the kind of people for whom others are thankful? Here are a few qualities that stand out:

- accepting others

- affirming others

- being real, not hypocritical

4

- being supportive
- being givers rather than takers

Paul remembered three qualities about the Thessalonians for which he was particularly grateful. Let's examine them in greater detail.

Remembering

> We give thanks to God always for all of you, . . .
> constantly bearing in mind your
> work of faith
> and labor of love
> and steadfastness of hope
> in our Lord Jesus Christ in the presence of our God
> and Father. (1 Thess. 1:2a, 3)

The Thessalonians' unseen attitudes of faith, love, and hope were like hidden roots that produced the fruit of good works, loving labor, and patient endurance.[6] How lush and fragrant these qualities were in Paul's memory now that he was so many miles away. He had come to Corinth "in weakness and in fear and in much trembling" (1 Cor. 2:3), but in his heart he carried with him a bouquet of encouragement, gathered from his brief encounter with the Thessalonian believers. Oh, how thankful he was for those memories!

He continues to reminisce in 1 Thessalonians 1:4 and 5:

> Knowing, brethren beloved by God, His choice of
> you; for our gospel did not come to you in word only,
> but also in power and in the Holy Spirit and with
> full conviction; just as you know what kind of men
> we proved to be among you for your sake.

The phrase "our gospel did not come to you in word only" reveals something of Paul's teaching method. He didn't fling the good news of Christ on each listener's doorstep and hurry on to the next house. Instead, he entered their homes and their hearts, imparting to them not only the gospel of God but also his own life (see also 2:8).

No wonder Paul was grateful for these beloved people! He had given them the gospel dressed in the servant garb of his own flesh,

---

6. In Greek, *steadfastness* is *hupomonē*, which literally means "to remain under," as a burro remains under its heavy load.

and the Thessalonians had embraced him . . . as well as his Lord.

Affirming

Paul affirms them for that warm reception, putting his arm around their shoulders and praising their progress since he left them.

> You also became imitators of us and of the Lord, having received the word in much tribulation with the joy of the Holy Spirit. (1:6)

Their welcoming of the gospel was twofold: first, they responded by imitating Paul's spiritual walk and the Lord's righteous example; second, they released their new beliefs into the world, to both Christians and non-Christians.

> You became an example to all the believers in Macedonia and in Achaia. For the word of the Lord has sounded forth from you, not only in Macedonia and Achaia, but also in every place your faith toward God has gone forth, so that we have no need to say anything.[7] (vv. 7–8)

As Paul moved through Macedonia, where Thessalonica was located, and Achaia, where Corinth was located, he would start to proclaim the gospel, then stop short in amazement. Still echoing down the canyons and through the streets was the word of the Lord spoken by the Thessalonian believers. Their Christianity was contagious and spreading faster than Paul could travel!

Reporting

We can imagine Paul, eager to tell the exciting news of the gospel's success in Thessalonica, beaten to the punch before he could utter a word:

> They themselves report about us what kind of a reception we had with you, and how you turned to God from idols to serve a living and true God, and to wait for His Son from heaven, whom He raised

---

7. The Greek word translated *sounded forth* could mean "sounding forth like *a trumpet*; the word could also mean crashing out like a *roll of thunder*. There is something tremendous about the sheer defiance of early Christianity." Barclay, *The Letters to the Philippians, Colossians, and Thessalonians*, p. 187.

from the dead, that is Jesus, who delivers us from
the wrath to come. (vv. 9–10)

As the reports spread farther and farther, Paul must have
laughed and marveled at these Thessalonians who had "turned to
God from idols." Now they had two purposes for their lives: "to
serve a living and true God" and "to wait for His Son from heaven."
They were exhibiting responsibility in the present yet readiness for
the future. They weren't anticipating the Lord's return so much that
they were neglecting the present, and they weren't becoming so
involved in their earthly responsibilities that they were forgetting
about the future.

This balance is an example of the lighthouse we mentioned
earlier. First Thessalonians is flashing its beacon and guiding us
between the rocks toward a committed Christian life.

Commitment: Challenge for a Growing Christian

The Thessalonian believers are already challenging us to a
three-way commitment—to the saved, to the unsaved, and to
Christ. First, we must be willing to accept and support others in
the family of God. Second, we must be involved with and available
for those without Christ. And third, we must be free of any en-
tanglements that pull us away from our Savior. These commitments
summarize the three basic priorities for our churches today. In a
nutshell, they describe a church and a people who have the right
stuff.

Living Insights   STUDY ONE

Paul and Silvanus and Timothy to the church
of the Thessalonians in God the Father and the Lord
Jesus Christ: Grace to you and peace. (1 Thess. 1:1)

Have you ever noticed that all of Paul's letters begin in nearly
the same way: "Grace to you and peace from God our Father and the
Lord Jesus Christ"? Take a few moments to look over Romans 1:7;
1 Corinthians 1:3; 2 Corinthians 1:2; Galatians 1:3; Ephesians 1:2;
Philippians 1:2; Colossians 1:2; 2 Thessalonians 1:2; 1 Timothy 1:2;
2 Timothy 1:2; Titus 1:4; and Philemon 1:3.

Why would Paul begin this way? Is there really any significance to it, or is this greeting just a convention, like our "Dear So-and-So"? Knowing Paul, it was no mere courtesy. It seems that before giving any instruction, any rebuke, any counsel, or any praise, he first took the time to center his readers in the heart of God.

And God's heart toward us, as Paul reveals it, overflows with grace and peace. Not judgment, wrath, condemnation, and scorn; but a kind and loving grace that freely gives us life and purpose and beauty, and a peace that comes from the security of being accepted by and belonging with Him.

So it seems fitting, as we embark on a study of Paul's letter, to follow his lead and first center ourselves in God's heart, then rest in His embrace.

Take a moment to put your name in 1 Thessalonians 1:1: "Paul and Silvanus and Timothy to _____ in God the Father and the Lord Jesus Christ: Grace to you and peace." Don't run by this, now. Stop and meditate on it, feel the meaning of it. Let the Spirit bring to mind other Scriptures illustrating God's heart of grace and peace.

What difference does realizing that He comes to you with grace make in your thinking?

_____

_____

_____

What insights do you gain in pondering that He desires peace for you?

_____

_____

_____

As we journey on through 1 Thessalonians, remember this lesson in God's love for you. And stay in the center of it always.

Living Insights   STUDY TWO

Paul thanked the Lord for the Thessalonian believers' "work of faith and labor of love and steadfastness of hope in our Lord Jesus

Christ" (v. 3). Let's carry these themes—faith, love, and hope—with us as we spend some time getting acquainted with the rest of Paul's letter.

Work of faith. Guided by the following verses, describe how the Thessalonians expressed their faith.

1:8 _____

1:9 _____

2:13 _____

3:5–8 _____

Labor of love. From these verses, describe the ways they showed and were instructed to show their love.

3:6 _____

3:12–13 _____

4:9–11 _____

5:12–13 _____

Steadfastness of hope. Write down how their hope was helping them endure hard times.

1:6–7, 9–10 _____

4:13–18 _____

5:8–11 _____

5:23–24 _____

If we think of faith, love, and hope as the three legs of a stool, which leg is weakest in your life right now? How can you strengthen that leg so that your foundation is sturdy and firm?

_____

_____

_____

1 THESSALONIANS: A HEART-TO-HEART TALK

Writer: Paul, the Apostle
Date: Early, about A.D. 50
Key Passages: 1:8–10; 4:9–11
Background: Acts 17:1–9

Unique Contributions:
- First of Paul's letters.
- Sets forth his style of ministry.
- Provides insight into the rapture of the church.
- Offers needed balance regarding the Lord's imminent return.
- Emphasis on vocational diligence.
- An excellent letter to use in getting others into personal Bible study.

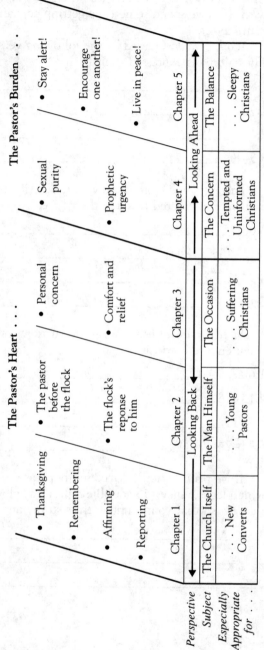

The Pastor's Heart . . .

- Thanksgiving
- Remembering
- Affirming
- Reporting

- The pastor before the flock
- The flock's reponse to him

- Personal concern
- Comfort and relief

The Pastor's Burden . . .

- Sexual purity
- Prophetic urgency

- Stay alert!
- Encourage one another!
- Live in peace!

Perspective	Looking Back			Looking Ahead	
	Chapter 1	Chapter 2	Chapter 3	Chapter 4	Chapter 5
Subject	The Church Itself	The Man Himself	The Occasion	The Concern	The Balance
Especially Appropriate for . . .	. . . New Converts	. . . Young Pastors	. . . Suffering Christians	. . . Tempted and Uninformed Christians	. . . Sleepy Christians

Chapter 2
A LEADERSHIP STYLE THAT WORKS . . . *GUARANTEED!*
1 Thessalonians 2:1–12

The sign over the building reads, "Al's Place—The Best Burgers in Town." In your mind flashes an image of a juicy beef patty on a bun, garnished with crisp lettuce and a hearty slice of tomato. Licking your lips, you step inside.

However, no host or hostess greets you—not even a sign inviting you to take a seat. After a few minutes, you seat yourself at the counter and wait. Eventually, a waitress emerges from the kitchen. Mashing the remainder of her break-time cigarette on the floor, she fishes through her apron for a stained order pad. "What'll ya have," she yawns, pulling a pencil from her hair. "Can I see a menu?" "Don't have menus," she says. "Oh. Well, I'll have a . . . hamburger."

She leaves for the kitchen.

You're considering heading for the front door, but the sign did say "The Best." So, still hopeful, you wait. After twenty minutes, she comes back. "Al says he forgot to order meat this week, but we got a little tuna left over. He can slap some on a bun, if ya want it."

◆

It doesn't take long to spot a poorly managed restaurant. From the food to the service, a restaurant reflects its leadership—or lack of it. The same is true for businesses, sports teams, churches, and even families. Good leadership is not optional; it's essential.

In this chapter, we'll be examining effective leadership traits modeled by the apostle Paul. As we prepare to study his example, let's begin with some thoughts about leadership and its definition.

A Brief Comment about Leadership

Simply put, leadership is "inspiring influence." It is the ability to ignite a blazing desire within people to do things they never imagined possible. It is rallying a defeated army to future victory or rousing apathetic students to astounding achievement. In a business, a good leader can stimulate high morale and willing sacrifice; in a family, strong character and lasting unity.

11

That is what leaders *do*. But it's not as easy to describe who leaders *are*. Neither is it as simple to define how leaders lead. In fact, equally effective leaders can have little in common. One successful sports coach may be gruff and hard-charging, while another may be contemplative and soft-spoken. Temperaments vary among leaders, as the shades and textures vary in different types of cloth. Yet one common thread appears to run through the fabric of them all: *leaders have the ability to get along well with people.*

In his book *The Making of a Christian Leader*, Ted Engstrom expands on this fact.

> The great American entrepreneur John D. Rockefeller stated, "I will pay more for the ability to deal with people than any other ability under the sun." According to a report by the American Management Association, an overwhelming majority of the two hundred managers who participated in a survey agreed that the most important single skill of an executive is [the] ability to get along with people. In the survey, management rated this ability more vital than intelligence, decisiveness, knowledge, or job skills.[1]

Isn't that interesting? Relational skills are more important to good leadership than temperament, technical prowess, or IQ. The apostle Paul illustrates this truth in the first twelve verses of the second chapter of 1 Thessalonians.

A Leadership Style Rarely Explained, Seldom Modeled

Although Paul spent only a short time starting the church in Thessalonica, it was still thriving a year later. How could he inspire such commitment for the Lord so quickly? Let's examine some of his leadership characteristics as he recounts with his own pen what happened.

Historical Background

As if he were sitting beside his readers paging through a photo album of his trip to Thessalonica, Paul recalls,

> For you yourselves know, brethren, that our coming to you was not in vain. (1 Thess. 2:1)

1. Ted W. Engstrom, *The Making of a Christian Leader* (Grand Rapids, Mich.: Zondervan Publishing House, 1976), p. 67.

"For you yourselves know," he says, pointing to one picture in their minds. "As you know . . . ," he writes a few sentences later, pointing to another (v. 5); "for you recall . . ." (v. 9), "you are witnesses . . ." (v. 10), "as you know . . ." (v. 11), he continues, turning the pages and reliving the experience with them. And what is it they know? That his coming to Thessalonica "was not in vain." The Greek word for *vain* here means "hollow, empty, wanting in purpose and earnestness."[2] Paul's visit had purpose and meaning; he had achieved real, substantial accomplishments. And lest anyone think they merely swung through town on a grand, self-promoting tour, Paul reminds us of what happened to him and Silas before they came to Thessalonica:

> But after we had already suffered and been mistreated in Philippi,[3] as you know, we had the boldness in our God to speak to you the gospel of God amid much opposition. (v. 2)

In Philippi, despite being Roman citizens, they had been publicly stripped and beaten and thrown into prison without a trial (Acts 16:19–24). It was an outrageous, humiliating injustice; yet, in the confidence of God, they pressed on and boldly preached His truth in Thessalonica.

Their scars of shame illustrate a significant principle about leadership: good leaders don't necessarily operate in ideal circumstances or come from trouble-free backgrounds. Bound by fear and guilt, we may feel disqualified by our pasts and unworthy of leadership. However, disabilities need not disqualify. Many times they can be a platform from which we can point others to the Lord. Struggling through pain, whether from abuse, a broken home, or personal failure, teaches us compassion and hope—two invaluable gifts any strong leader will wish to impart.

---

2. J. B. Lightfoot, as quoted by Fritz Rienecker in *A Linguistic Key to the Greek New Testament*, ed. Cleon L. Rogers, Jr. (Grand Rapids, Mich.: Zondervan Publishing House, Regency Reference Library, 1980), p. 588.

3. The Greek word for *mistreated* "expresses insulting and outrageous treatment and [especially] treatment which is calculated publicly to insult and openly to humiliate the person who suffers from it." Rienecker, *Linguistic Key to Greek New Testament*, p. 588.

Some Negatives: Things to Omit

Out of his own pain, Paul appeals to the Thessalonians with a leadership style that intentionally avoids four negative traits. First, *he was not deceptive.*

> For our exhortation does not come from error or impurity or by way of deceit. (1 Thess. 2:3)

Paul didn't show up at their doorstep tipping his hat and offering them a deal with a money-back guarantee. His message was simple and up-front. Without any ulterior motives, he spoke to them as a man of integrity.

Second, *he was not a people pleaser.*

> Just as we have been approved by God to be entrusted with the gospel, so we speak, not as pleasing men but God, who examines our hearts. (v. 4)

Although leaders must be able to get along well with people, they must avoid becoming people pleasers. Because people pleasers are motivated by insecurity, when controversial issues arise, they try to sit on both sides of the fence instead of making the necessary decisions. To keep peace, they hedge on the truth; to duck criticism, they say what people want to hear. In the end, though, they lose the respect of others—and themselves.

Paul, however, avoids this trap, reminding the Thessalonians that he "never came with flattering speech, as you know" (v. 5a). He determined, in word and deed, to please God alone (see also Gal. 1:10). Of course, this perspective doesn't imply that we can thumb our noses at people or, worse yet, run them over in the name of truth. Rather, it gives us confidence to do what is right before God and let public opinion fall where it may.

Third, *he was not greedy.*

> For we never came . . . with a pretext for greed— God is witness.[4] (1 Thess. 2:5)

Greed is the consuming desire to have more than we need and to yearn for the possessions of others. Often, we associate greed with money, but for Christian leaders, other seemingly noble pursuits can wear greed's shadowy cape and hood—pursuits such as

---

4. Flattery is evident to all, but only "God is witness" of our hidden greed.

higher church attendance, more converts, or bigger buildings. Through self-control and God's scrutiny, Paul was able to excise greed from his heart, and God Himself testified that his motives were pure.

Fourth, *he was not authoritarian.*

> Nor did we seek glory from men, either from you or from others, even though as apostles of Christ we might have asserted our authority. (v. 6)

Although Paul, as an apostle, had the right to demand first-class treatment, he didn't take advantage of that privilege. Instead, he humbly served the Thessalonians.

Abusing authority is a particularly powerful temptation for spiritual leaders, because their position, their verbal ability, and their knowledge of Scripture can awe people. Followers who tend to pedestalize their leaders may feel obligated to protect them and allow them great authority. Leaders soon discover that they can get away with being bossy, but that's not modeling a servant's attitude. Servants know themselves well enough to put the brakes on their authority when pride starts to take control.

Some Positives: Things to Include

As a servant-leader, Paul also models four positive traits of effective leadership. The first characteristic is *sensitivity to needs.*

> But we proved to be gentle among you, as a nursing mother tenderly cares for her own children. (v. 7)

Like a nursing mother, Paul gently and tenderly cradled these infant believers, nourishing them with his own life and the pure milk of God's Word (see 1 Pet. 2:2). Selflessly, he committed himself to understanding their hopes and fears so he could meet their deepest needs. Such sensitive leadership cannot happen from a distance; it requires personal involvement and love.

The second trait is *affection for people.* "Having thus a fond affection for you . . . you had become very dear to us" (1 Thess. 2:8a, c). Sensing Paul's love for them, the believers didn't feel used or manipulated; Paul wasn't tossing them from one objective to another. And they could get close to him—he didn't maintain a "professional distance." They could draw near and see compassion in his eyes.

Third, Paul models *transparency and authenticity of life.*

We were well-pleased to impart to you not only the gospel of God but also our own lives. . . . For you recall, brethren, our labor and hardship, how working night and day so as not to be a burden to any of you, we proclaimed to you the gospel of God. You are witnesses, and so is God, how devoutly and uprightly and blamelessly we behaved toward you believers.[5] (vv. 8b, 9–10)

The Apostle incarnated the gospel in the reality of his own life. He opened up his secrets, his struggles, his scars, his humanity— and he worked hard to live out the principles he was trying to preach. Only when your message meshes with your actions do you have the power to impart life.

And his fourth characteristic is *enthusiastic affirmation*.

Just as you know how we were exhorting and encouraging and imploring each one of you as a father would his own children. (v. 11)

Like an enthusiastic dad rooting for his football-player son, Paul cheered on the Thessalonians. How much do we Christians need this kind of affirmation! We've been beaten with our unworthiness and sinfulness until we're black and blue. We need to know that we're in Christ and it's His righteousness God sees, that there is hope for sinners, a future for failures, forgiveness for saints. We've got to stop shooting our own wounded and encourage and affirm them instead.

The Ultimate Objective

Paul didn't exhort the Thessalonians so they would become trophies in the display case of his ego. Instead, his goal was this:

So that you may walk in a manner worthy of the God who calls you into His own kingdom and glory. (v. 12)

Paul's leadership style focused on the benefit of those he served— that they might follow the Lord and enjoy His presence forever.

---

5. Notice Paul's integrity in these verses. He not only "proclaimed" (v. 9), he also "devoutly and uprightly and blamelessly . . . behaved" (v. 10). He imparted truth through living a life that was true.

Three Essential Qualities

Having examined Paul's leadership traits, you may discover that it is one thing to read about them and yet another to make them a part of your life. Here are three words of advice that will help you as you begin.

- *Look within:* Develop an inner security that will guard you from becoming a people pleaser and keep you confident in the Lord.

- *Look around:* Commit yourself to excellence in all you do. Determine a vision for your life and follow it.

- *Look up:* Maintain a deliberate and practical faith that takes the initiative in seeking and obeying God.

With your heart in focus and your gaze set unwaveringly on your goal, Paul's positive, practical leadership can be carried out in your life.

Living Insights   STUDY ONE

As we have seen, temperament has little to do with being an effective leader. What does determine success in leadership, though, are the eight traits Paul modeled. Try rating yourself in light of them, to explore your strengths and weaknesses.

- Do I manipulate people through deception or model God's way with integrity?

    1   2   3   4   5

    Deception/Manipulation   Integrity/Modeling

- Am I motivated by a longing to please people or to please God?

    1   2   3   4   5

    People pleaser   Pleaser of God

- In my heart, is greed influencing my actions or am I controlling that tendency?

    1   2   3   4   5

    Greedy   Self-controlled

- Am I likely to take advantage of my authority or am I willing to give up privileges and serve others?

  1   2   3   4   5

  Authoritarian   Servant-hearted

- Am I unaware of people's problems or am I sensitive to their needs?

  1   2   3   4   5

  Unaware   Sensitive

- Do I come across as indifferent or affectionate toward those around me?

  1   2   3   4   5

  Indifferent   Affectionate

- Do I tend to hold people at arm's length or do I let them see me as I really am?

  1   2   3   4   5

  Distant/Closed   Transparent/Authentic

- Do others find me critical and complaining or supportive and encouraging?

  1   2   3   4   5

  Judgmental   Affirming

From this general picture, how can you better help those you lead "walk in a manner worthy of the God who calls" them (1 Thess. 2:12)?

_____

_____

_____

_____

_____

_____

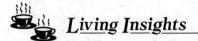 *Living Insights* STUDY TWO

Whether pastors, parents, or company presidents, the most influential Christian leaders impart not only the truth but their lives as well. However, this human side of leadership is often neglected.

> The popular yet mistaken mental image of a successful leader is the tough-minded executive who is always in control, who holds himself aloof, who operates in a world of untouchable, sophisticated secrecy. If he or she has needs, feels alone, wrestles with very human problems, lacks the ability to cope with some particular pressure . . . no one should ever know about it. And *certainly* there is no place for tears! That would be a sign of weakness, and real leaders don't cry . . . nor do they evidence any other emotion than a self-assured air of confidence.[6]

Your followers may be the children in your home, the employees at the office, or your friends at church. In what ways can you break the barrier of "sophisticated secrecy" and impart your life to them?

Offer the truth with a little seasoning of humanity. Weep with your followers, rejoice with them—don't be afraid of being vulnerable. Your life is the greatest leadership tool you possess.

---

6. Charles R. Swindoll, *Leadership: Influence That Inspires* (Waco, Tex.: Word Books, 1985), pp. 59–60.

Chapter 3

THE FLIP SIDE OF
LEADERSHIP
1 Thessalonians 2:13–20

A leader without followers is like Arturo Toscanini without an orchestra. He may tap his baton on the music stand, lift his hands dramatically, and drop them for the downbeat; but without musicians, he is merely a man waving his hands without purpose.

However, give him an orchestra to direct—a group of followers skilled in their instruments and dedicated to his leadership—and he is no longer a man vainly beating the air. He is a maestro.

Successful leading depends on responsive following; it is the "flip side" of leadership. As strong as Paul's leadership qualities were—he avoided deception, people pleasing, greed, and authoritarianism while cultivating sensitivity, affection, authenticity, and affirmation—they would all have been gestures in the wind if the Thessalonians hadn't followed his lead.

As we examine 1 Thessalonians 2:13–20, let's listen for some of the qualities of a good follower, beginning with the one characteristic for which Paul was most thankful.

The Reason for Gratitude

> For this reason we also constantly thank God that when you received from us the word of God's message, you accepted it not as the word of men, but for what it really is, the word of God, which also performs its work in you who believe. (2:13)

How grateful Paul was that these people not only listened to the message as God's Word, but they swung open their hearts and embraced it warmly as a cherished guest.[1] Nothing could have

---

1. Paul uses two Greek words to describe the Thessalonians' response to the gospel: *paralambanō* for *received* and *dechomai* for *accepted*. "The [first] word for receiving is one that denotes an objective, outward receiving. . . . The second word for receiving denotes rather a subjective reception, a reception that involves welcome and approval (the word is the usual one for the reception of a guest . . .)." Leon Morris, *The First and Second Epistles to the Thessalonians,* rev. ed., The New International Commentary on the New Testament series (Grand Rapids, Mich.: William B. Eerdmans Publishing Co., 1991), pp. 80–81.

encouraged the Apostle more than this spirit of welcome, this ready acceptance of God's truth. For Paul knew that the power was in the Word, not in him. As F. F. Bruce writes,

> The word of human beings, however wise in substance or eloquent in expression, cannot produce spiritual life: this is the prerogative of the word of God.[2]

As that spiritual life began to blossom within the believers, certain changes in attitude began to bear fruit. Let's take a look at some of those changes, as well as how those new attitudes in turn affected their leader Paul.

The Responses in Attitude

The Thessalonians beautifully illustrate the principle that when God's Word is welcomed, God's working is evident. We can observe three godly evidences of their faith in Christ as they followed Paul's leadership.

Among Those Being Led

The first response was *cooperation with needed changes*. The Thessalonian church was made up of Jews, God-fearing Greeks, and formerly idolatrous pagans. From such varied backgrounds, these people had had the Word planted in their hearts. Over time and through afflictions, it had begun to "perform its work," pushing up seedlings of change in their lives (v. 13b).

Their part was not to grit their teeth and force themselves to grow but to cooperate with the changes occurring within. The Word, not their own initiative, was altering their attitudes and perceptions, providing the power for change.[3]

As a result of the truth working in their lives, the Thessalonians began showing signs of a second response: *imitation of a godly lifestyle*.

> For you, brethren, became imitators of the churches of God in Christ Jesus that are in Judea. (v. 14a)

2. F. F. Bruce, *Word Biblical Commentary: 1 and 2 Thessalonians* (Waco, Tex.: Word Books, 1982), vol. 45, p. 45.

3. Writing to Timothy, Paul describes the work Scripture performs in our lives—teaching, reproving, correcting, and training us in righteousness, "that the man of God may be adequate, equipped for every good work" (2 Tim. 3:16–17).

The book of Acts describes the resiliency and dedication of the churches in Judea—where Christianity had begun (see Acts 2–7). Paul complimented the Thessalonian believers by telling them they were just like those churches. How did they know what the Judean churches were like? Had they been watching a film series on the suffering Christians in Jerusalem?

No, of course not. The connection between the churches was their common goal. As each group was moving toward godliness, the Holy Spirit was moving them toward each other. In this way, two groups of people separated by hundreds of miles and living in different cultures were imitating each other by imitating the life of Christ.

A third response of these followers was *endurance through intense suffering*. Not only did they share the destination of godliness, they also met the same dangers along the way.

> For you also endured the same sufferings [as the Judean believers] at the hands of your own country-men, even as they did from the Jews, who both killed the Lord Jesus and the prophets, and drove us out. They are not pleasing to God, but hostile to all men, hindering us from speaking to the Gentiles that they might be saved; with the result that they always fill up the measure of their sins. But wrath has come upon them to the utmost. (1 Thess. 2:14b–16)

There are many differences among Christians around the world, but there is one thing we all share: suffering.

Personally, Paul felt such a bond between himself and the Thessalonians. Their own people were turning against them just as his own people had turned against him. In fact, these antagonists came from the same poisoned spring that spawned the crucifiers of Jesus and murderers of the prophets. They all shared wounds from a common enemy—an enemy whom God will eventually conquer at the Last Judgment.[4]

With these words, Paul was encouraging his followers to continue standing firm. He and they were in this struggle together, and

---

4. Paul says these hostile opponents "always fill up the measure of their sins" (v. 16b). F. F. Bruce explains, "Their cup of guilt was already well on the way to being filled, and their present conduct was filling it up to the brim. . . . They have reached the point of no return in their opposition to the gospel and final, irremediable retribution is inevitable; indeed it has come." *1 and 2 Thessalonians*, p. 48.

no matter what happened, God was in control. There is peace in knowing that although the winds may roar and the lightning crack and the seas swell, things are not out of God's hands.

Within the Leader Himself

Followers who respond so courageously and with such commitment to the Lord inspire their leaders, motivating them to a higher level of service. It is true: a responsive attitude in one group breeds an equally responsive attitude in the other. Hence, as Paul shifts subjects in the next verse to his companions and himself, we notice three ways leaders respond to their followers.

Their first response is an *eager expectation in spite of separation.*

But we, brethren, having been bereft of you for
a short while—in person, not in spirit—were all
the more eager with great desire to see your face.
(1 Thess. 2:17)

The Greek word for *bereft* means "to make one an orphan by separation."[5] Like a father whose children had been torn away from him and abandoned on the streets in a faraway city, Paul longed to rush to the believers and gather them in his arms. Real love grows between leaders and their followers as the relationship between them deepens.

Second, there is *a constant pursuit amidst satanic opposition.*

For we wanted to come to you—I, Paul, more than
once—and yet Satan thwarted us. (v. 18)

Paul felt Satan was keeping him from fulfilling his dream of returning to Thessalonica. The Greek word *egkoptō*, translated here as *thwart*, has a fascinating history that adds weight to Paul's meaning.

The word was originally used of breaking up a road
to render it impassable and later it was used in a
military sense of making a break through the enemy's
line. It was also used in the athletic sense of cutting
in on someone during a race.[6]

---

5. Fritz Rienecker, A Linguistic Key to the Greek New Testament, ed. Cleon L. Rogers, Jr. (Grand Rapids, Mich.: Zondervan Publishing House, Regency Reference Library, 1980), p. 593.

6. Rienecker, A Linguistic Key, p. 593.

Satan tries to break up our path or cut in on our stride to trip us up. It is sometimes difficult to perceive satanic involvement in our lives, so we must learn to be sensitive to his influence. Being persistent and standing firm in the Spirit and the Word will help in gaining the upper hand against the devil (see Eph. 6:13). For as John promised: "Greater is He who is in you than he who is in the world" (1 John 4:4b).

Paul's third response as leader was *a joyful hope undiminished by problems*.

> For who is our hope or joy or crown of exultation?
> Is it not even you, in the presence of our Lord Jesus
> at His coming? For you are our glory and joy.
> (1 Thess. 2:19–20)

He could have focused on his problems—that he felt torn away from his friends and cut off from seeing them again. He could have sat in Corinth, stewing in the juices of self-pity and loneliness. But Paul instead lifted his eyes toward heaven and reveled in the hope of Christ's glorious coming. Standing in His presence, he imagined himself side by side with these spiritual children whom he had watched being born into God's family. They were his pride and joy; and nothing could diminish his hopeful anticipation of seeing them again, if not in this life, then in the one to come.

When the problems of this world threaten to overwhelm us, we sometimes respond by hunching our shoulders and wearing a grim, sackcloth-and-ashes expression. "I'm doomed. My circumstances will never change, my life will never improve, and no one cares."

It is easy to lose our hope, our humor, and our hunger for spiritual things. With white knuckles, we grip the reins of our Christian life, driving ourselves from one activity to the next. Our witnessing becomes intense and overbearing; our worship becomes lifeless. That's when we need to remind ourselves of what is truly important—the Lord and people. It's OK to dismount, walk awhile, and enjoy the relationships we'll have for eternity.

Hearing and Doing

In this chapter, we've picked out a lot of principles concerning followers and leaders. To keep them from being scattered in our minds, let's organize them into two categories: what we've heard and what we can do about it.

What We've Heard	What We Can Do
An attitude of gratitude can be developed by welcoming God's truth.	I will welcome the truth I hear.
A commitment to contentment will be strengthened by accepting God's will.	I will accept the path I walk.
A happiness amidst heaviness must be cultivated by affirming God's people.	I will affirm the people I love.

"For you are our glory and joy," wrote Paul, pouring out his heart to his followers in love and affirmation. Who is your glory and joy? Let them know today.

Living Insights

STUDY ONE

The Thessalonian believers not only received the Word, but they welcomed it into their hearts. Sometimes for us the distance between our minds and hearts seems like a long road to travel. We hear the truth, but it may take a while before we welcome it.

We hear, for example, "The Lord protects the strangers; He supports the fatherless and the widow" (Ps. 146:9a). But perhaps we don't actually welcome that truth until a tragedy occurs: a husband dies or a father leaves. Suddenly, the Word is at our heart's door, and we embrace it in a tearful reunion.

We'd like to reacquaint your heart with a few verses, one of which may particularly apply to your current circumstances. Meditate on that verse, welcome it with open arms, and take a few moments to express how that truth will encourage you this week.

Psalm 34:4–7	2 Corinthians 4:16–18
Psalm 37:7–11	Colossians 2:13–14
Habakkuk 3:17–19	1 Peter 1:6–9
Matthew 6:31–34	Revelation 21:3–4

"I'm late. I'm behind. Gotta get there. Gotta keep moving. Stupid drivers keep getting in my way."

Honk! Honk!

"Where'd you learn to drive?! I'm late. I'm behind. Gotta get there. Gotta keep moving."

For some Christians, life is a constant drive through rush-hour traffic. There are deadlines at work, meetings at church, and chores at home; appointments to keep and people to meet, problems to solve and money to stretch. And the Christian responsibilities never ease up: being a good witness, teaching Sunday school, serving on a committee. Who has time to exit this freeway? "I'm late. I'm behind. Gotta get there. Gotta keep moving!"

Has your life felt like a rush-hour drive lately? Accelerating from one responsibility to the next, have you been changing lanes so fast that you're whizzing by people without even noticing them? Look in the mirror—do you see a grim, determined, get-it-done-at-all-costs expression on your face? Have you lost your hope, your sense of humor, and your spiritual hunger?

Time for a rest stop.

Jesus said, "My yoke is easy, and My load is light." He really did—it's in Matthew 11:30! Have you possibly added weight to His yoke to make it a burden? If so, in what ways?

_____

_____

_____

_____

How can you lighten your load?

_____

_____

_____

Despite his problems in Corinth, Paul found joy in his relationship with the Thessalonians. In what ways can you focus more on enjoying relationships and less on tasks this week?

_____

_____

_____

Some of your busyness may be unavoidable. In what ways can you restore your hope, humor, and spiritual hunger during your busy day?

_____

_____

_____

The devil will do all he can to make you overtired, overcommitted, and overbusy. In the space provided, set some priorities for your work, home, and church life that will guard you from driving too much in the fast lane.

_____

_____

_____

Chapter 4

WHEN YOUR COMFORT ZONE GETS THE SQUEEZE

1 Thessalonians 3:1–8

Imagine stacking up all the poems and essays ever written about the wonders of romantic love. How high would the pile reach? Would it be as tall as the Empire State Building? As high as Mount Everest? Now add to the stack the works on valor and patriotism and family. Who can count them all?

But look around for a flowing lyric on the topic of pain. You won't find many! Writer Philip Yancey acknowledges,

> I have never read a poem extolling the virtues of pain, nor seen a statue erected in its honor, nor heard a hymn dedicated to it. Pain is usually defined as "unpleasantness."
>
> Christians don't really know how to interpret pain. If you pinned them against the wall, in a dark, secret moment, many Christians would probably admit that pain was God's one mistake. He really should have worked a little harder and invented a better way of coping with the world's dangers.[1]

Pain and its companions—affliction, suffering, hardship, and adversity—are often seen as the invading enemies of life. Whenever we spy one coming at us, we usually turn and run. We tend to think life should be fair and straightforward, so when our comfort zones get the squeeze, we feel angry. Yet according to the Bible, pain is a necessary part of life. And although we may not like it, we can learn to live with it.

To Set the Record Straight

There's a tension involved in trying to accept the pain that God allows while, at the same time, fighting to overcome it. But,

---

1. Philip Yancey, *Where Is God When It Hurts?* (Grand Rapids, Mich.: Zondervan Publishing House, 1977), pp. 22–23.

like the Thessalonians, we can find real help in our struggle when we learn to see pain from His perspective. His Word reveals that suffering is both inevitable and essential.

Suffering Is Inevitable

Paul told the Philippian believers:

> For to you it has been granted for Christ's sake, not only to believe in Him, but also to suffer for His sake. (Phil. 1:29)

Some advocates of the health-and-wealth gospel teach that if Christians have enough faith, they won't suffer. But Paul says suffering walks hand in hand with faith in Christ. They're part of the same package that God has granted us while we live in this world.[2]

To the Corinthians, Paul described the details of his own suffering:

> Afflicted in every way, but not crushed; perplexed, but not despairing; persecuted, but not forsaken; struck down, but not destroyed; always carrying about in the body the dying of Jesus, that the life of Jesus also may be manifested in our body. (2 Cor. 4:8–10)

We *always* carry in our bodies "the dying of Jesus"—His pain and suffering, which is manifested in our own afflictions and persecutions. By bearing up under the deathlike lifestyle of pain, we actually enter into the lifestyle of Christ—which, paradoxically, is real living. It's one of the mysteries of God.

Because suffering so often takes us off guard, Peter advises,

> Beloved, do not be surprised at the fiery ordeal among you, which comes upon you for your testing, as though some strange thing were happening to you; but to the degree that you share the sufferings of Christ, keep on rejoicing; so that also at the revelation of His glory, you may rejoice with exultation. If you are reviled for the name of Christ, you are blessed, because the Spirit of glory and of God rests upon you. (1 Pet. 4:12–14)

---

2. God isn't the author of evil or the cause of evil actions against us (compare 1 John 1:5). Sin is the bitter root of the pain and violence that has infested our world (see Rom. 8:20–22).

A soldier is not surprised by hardship and enemy attacks; neither should we think it strange when Christ's enemies revile us. Instead, we can rejoice that our Captain finds us worthy to suffer alongside Him.

Pain Is Essential

Suffering is not only inevitable, the pain it brings is essential to our growth in two ways. First, according to the psalmist, afflictions act as tutors, teaching us lessons about God and His Word we would never learn otherwise.

> Before I was afflicted I went astray,
> But now I keep Thy word. . . .
> It is good for me that I was afflicted,
> That I may learn Thy statutes. . . .
> I know, O Lord, that Thy judgments are righteous,
> And that in faithfulness Thou hast afflicted me.
> (Ps. 119:67, 71, 75)

Second, according to Solomon, adversity slows us down and sensitizes us to God.

> Consider the work of God,
> For who is able to straighten what He has bent?
> In the day of prosperity be happy,
> But in the day of adversity consider—
> God has made the one as well as the other
> So that man may not discover anything that will
> be after him. (Eccles. 7:13–14)

The Hebrew word for *consider* refers to "mental observation" and means "inquire into . . . give attention to . . . reflect."[3] Affliction makes us put on the brakes and carefully examine where we're going and why we're going there. It reveals the truth about the nature of ourselves and the nature of God, who allows both prosperity and hardship to enter our lives.

Take the Thessalonians, for Example

One group of people who were finding out firsthand about pain's

---

3. William Gesenius, *A Hebrew and English Lexicon of the Old Testament*, trans. Edward Robinson, ed. Francis Brown, S. R. Driver, and Charles A. Briggs (1906; reprint, Oxford, England: Clarendon Press, 1951), p. 907.

realities were the Thessalonians. As we pick up Paul's line of thought in 1 Thessalonians 3, let's examine how he responds to their sufferings and what he can teach us during our own difficult days.

Relational Concern

You will recall that a wave of persecution had forced the Apostle away from the Christians in Thessalonica. As he traveled to other cities, he worried about these new believers like a parent who tosses and turns in the night, concerned about his faraway children. Finally, while visiting Athens before coming to Corinth, he took action.

> Therefore when we could endure it no longer, we thought it best to be left behind at Athens alone; and we sent Timothy, our brother and God's fellow worker in the gospel of Christ, to strengthen and encourage you as to your faith. (1 Thess. 3:1–2)

Timothy's twofold instructions were "to strengthen and encourage." The Greek word for *strengthen* means "to support . . . to establish. The word has the idea of putting in a buttress as a support."[4] Like a stone buttress, Timothy attached himself to the Thessalonian believers, keeping them from shifting and buckling. Using hope as his mortar and truth as his stones, he built up sturdy columns upon which the people could lean when harsh winds blew.

In addition, Paul told Timothy to encourage them as to their faith. In Greek, this word is *parakaleō*, which is a combination of two words: *para*, "beside"; and *kaleō*, "to call." Together they mean "to cheer, encourage, comfort."[5] Timothy was called alongside the people to keep their faith strong in their most difficult hour.

The Thessalonians must have felt like the fugitive David, whom King Saul hunted in the wilderness. They too sensed their persecutors' dogged presence at every turn. Then came Timothy, like the faithful Jonathan, who "arose and went to David at Horesh, and encouraged him in God" (1 Sam. 23:16). How David must have treasured Jonathan's brotherly support, and equally so, how precious Timothy's comfort must have been to the Thessalonians!

4. Fritz Rienecker, A Linguistic Key to the Greek New Testament, ed. Cleon L. Rogers, Jr. (Grand Rapids, Mich.: Zondervan Publishing House, Regency Reference Library, 1980), p. 594.

5. G. Abbott-Smith, A Manual Greek Lexicon of the New Testament, 3d ed. (Edinburgh, Scotland: T. and T. Clark, 1937), p. 340.

Do you know a "David," someone being hunted in the wilderness of suffering or persecution? Maybe someone new in the faith whose face keeps appearing before your mind's eye? Images of the Thessalonians kept flashing through Paul's mind until he could endure it no longer. He was deeply concerned that "the tempter might have tempted you, and our labor should be in vain" (1 Thess. 3:5). If you feel this kind of churning uneasiness for a fellow believer, send help as Paul did or go personally like Timothy or Jonathan. Don't ignore those churnings; follow up on them instead.

Theological Perspective

To shore up the Thessalonians' faith, Paul needed to impart a proper theological perspective on suffering, which he unveils in verses 3 and 4.

> [We sent Timothy] so that no man may be disturbed by these afflictions; for you yourselves know that we have been destined for this. For indeed when we were with you, we kept telling you in advance that we were going to suffer affliction; and so it came to pass, as you know.

"Don't let afflictions *disturb* you," Paul says. That word in Greek, *sainō*, is used only here in all the New Testament. It means "to wag the tail," as a dog does. Paul, probably playing on the word, was saying, "Don't be misled by the tail's wagging." An affliction is much like a tail-wagging dog, which from a distance looks easy to handle. When approached, however, the dog snarls and viciously snaps at your hand. In a similar manner, the Apostle didn't want the Thessalonians, in the midst of this "tail-wagging" trial, to be bitten, shaken, and hurt. A child of God does not need to be unsettled by affliction.

While suffering hard times, we can easily be disturbed by questions that shake us to the core. "Doesn't God care about me anymore? Didn't He promise to help me? How can a good God let this happen?" We begin to question God's love for us and wonder if we've believed wrongly all our lives. This is exactly why Paul sent Timothy: to strengthen and encourage the believers so that doubts wouldn't capsize their faith in the midst of affliction.

To further protect his readers, Paul reminds them and us about two facts: first, "you yourselves know that we have been destined for this" (v. 3b). Just as Christ was destined for the Cross, so we also have our own crosses to bear. They are a part of God's training program for our lives.

Second, Paul writes, "We kept telling you in advance that we were going to suffer affliction" (v. 4a). Knowing ahead of time that persecution and affliction are on their way helps us prepare ourselves, just as soldiers forewarned of an enemy attack can better defend themselves. On the other hand, if we refuse to believe the warnings and assume that trusting Christ will solve all our earthly problems, we're setting ourselves up for a Pearl Harbor-type raid. Such an attack will not only shock us, it can devastate us as well.

Personal Response

The aftermath of this kind of spiritual devastation might leave a threefold response in our hearts: (1) resentment toward a former or current authority figure, (2) isolation from Christian friends, (3) indifference toward biblical teaching. To Paul's relief, the Thessalonians showed no signs of any of these bitter reactions. Instead, from the following verses, we can observe the opposite responses:

> But now that Timothy has come to us from you, and
> has brought us good news of your faith and love, and
> that you always think kindly of us, longing to see us
> just as we also long to see you, for this reason, breth-
> ren, in all our distress and affliction we were com-
> forted about you through your faith. (vv. 6–7)

First, they refused to blame their former authority figures, for Paul wrote, "you always think kindly of us." Second, they desired to maintain close ties with their Christian friends—"[you long] to see us just as we also long to see you." And third, they committed themselves to spiritual truth—"we were comforted about you through your faith."

We can imagine that Paul slept much easier after hearing Timothy's report about the Thessalonians. What a burden had been lifted from his soul!

"For now we really live," Paul writes, encouraging them with a final exhortation, "if you stand firm in the Lord" (v. 8). He knew that they would be all right. Nobody could force God out of Thessalonica . . . or out of their hearts.

Now That We Understand

In the wake of Paul's words about suffering are two rippling waves of truth for us today.

Having our comfort zone invaded as Christians is essential, not unfair. Although author Philip Yancey rightly observes that pain is "the gift nobody wants,"[6] it is the gift everybody must open in order to grow. When it lands on your doorstep, don't be afraid to unwrap it. For it contains never-to-be-forgotten lessons about life.

Suffering hardship as soldiers in battle is expected, not unusual. Back in the days of World War II, the saying "There's a war on!" signaled everybody's awareness of the need for sacrifice. Likewise, as long as this world is our home, we need to remember that we're in enemy territory. So stay prepared, and stand firm in the Lord.

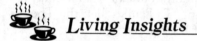 *Living Insights* STUDY ONE

Put yourself in Timothy's sandals. Paul has sent you to strengthen and encourage the faith of a group of suffering Christians. Several have lost their jobs because of their faith. Others tell of being ostracized from their families. Their church meetings must be held in secret because of brutality from intolerant city officials. Now they are looking to you for strength, for hope . . . what would you say?

Take some time to reread the verses on suffering quoted in the lesson. Based on these passages, summarize some of the principles you would try to explain to these persecuted people.

_____

_____

_____

Now think about someone in your life who is suffering. In what ways can you be a Timothy to this person? Based on what you've just written, what can you say to strengthen and encourage him or her? What can you do?

_____

6. Yancey, *Where Is God When It Hurts?*, p. 21.

34

Like Paul, we send you to the Thessalonians in your world. Certainly, Timothy's sandals are not easy to fill; it takes compassion, tact, and effort. But in God's power, you can be a terrific Timothy!

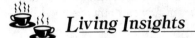

Living Insights

During your hard times, what weedlike doubts take root in your mind? Mark the ones from the list below or write in your own.

❑ How can God be loving and allow this pain in my life?

❑ Is God too busy or uncaring to answer my prayers?

❑ Does God really exist?

❑ _____

As a result of these thoughts, have you ever resented your authority figures? Isolated yourself from Christian friends? Or felt indifferent toward biblical teaching? If so, in what ways?

_____

_____

_____

How can knowing that "we have been destined for this" (1 Thess. 3:3b) and that pain is essential for maturity guard you against these reactions?

_____

_____

_____

Chapter 5

WHAT DOES IT MEAN TO "REALLY LIVE"?

1 Thessalonians 3:9–13

W hat does it mean to "really live"? Some people say, "It takes money to really live, because money can buy the good life." But is "the good life" the same as "the real life"?

Some people say, "Real living belongs to the vibrant young." So, smoothing out our wrinkles, tucking in our tummies, and combing our hair over our bald spots, we do what we can to stay young and not fall behind in the fast lane of youth. But is "the fast life" the same as "the real life"?

"A life of comfort and ease—swingin' in a hammock and sippin' lemonade under a shade tree—that's living!" Yet, do we truly think a sleepy, pampered life is "the real life"? How about the educated life or the productive life or the organized life? Do any of these pursuits define what it means to "really live"?

If we asked God that question, He'd probably shake His head no—none of that constitutes real living. Unfortunately, humankind rarely turns to Him for His thoughts on the matter, even though He is our Maker. Instead, as Solomon points out, we tend to seek out "many devices" of our own to make us happy (Eccles. 7:29b).[1] We substitute the artificial for the authentic, the phony for the real—particularly in three areas.

Left to Ourselves, We Substitute

First, *mentally, we substitute knowledge for wisdom.* Many times, we are more impressed by scholarship and the opinions of experts than by divine understanding. The latest research tends to hold more sway than "old-fashioned" biblical principles. It's the clever people debating new theories who attract the media, not common folks teaching godly wisdom.

---

1. The Hebrew word for *devices* comes from the root verb, "to think." The New International Version translates the word as *schemes.* The idea is to think through a strategy and arrange clever or imaginative plans.

Second, *emotionally, we substitute feelings for facts.* We're more prone these days to believe what feels right rather than what the facts say is right. For example, the rising rates of drug abuse and unwed mothers illustrate how hard it is in our society to "just say no" to things that feel good, even though the facts point to the serious and often harmful consequences of our actions.

Third, *spiritually, we substitute the temporal for the eternal.* This is the most harmful of the three substitutes because we cling to what won't last and let go of what will. So often we give our lives to the urgent rather than the important, to knowing the cost of things but not their real value, to pursuing what we can see and measure and feel right now instead of the deeper spiritual realities we'll live with forever.

Thankfully, we are not left entirely to ourselves to discover the real life, because God has given us His perspective in His Word. Life's artificial substitutes may usher us into a world of wishes, fantasy, and futility, but God's Word reveals a land of meaning, truth, and reality. The latter is the land in which Paul lived, as we can see through his joyful response to the Thessalonians' firm faith: "For now we really live" (1 Thess. 3:8a). Let's journey through that realm with him and discover God's idea of what it means to really live.

Listening to God, We Change

"Now we're really livin'!" probably would not have been the first words out of our mouths if we had been in Paul's situation at the time he wrote 1 Thessalonians. Miles from home, plagued with poor health, and hounded by enemies, he was enduring constant hardships. But because of four factors in his life, he could experience God's perspective on real living.

Joyful in Gratitude

The first factor appears in verse 9:

> For what thanks can we render to God for you in return for all the joy with which we rejoice before our God on your account . . . ?

Do you have friends who are so accepting and loving that just thinking about them warms you inside like a cup of hot chocolate on a gray winter day? This was the kind of friendship Paul had with the Thessalonians. As he drank in his memories of them, he could rejoice in spite of the cold winds of "distress and affliction" and satanic hindrances that kept him from joining them (v. 7; 2:18). Out of that joy came overflowing gratitude to the Lord.

Paul thankfully counted God's blessings in his life—blessings that included the Thessalonians first of all. Deep within him was his simple philosophy of real living: be joyful in gratitude. He could say wholeheartedly, like the psalmist,

> Bless the Lord, O my soul;
> And all that is within me, bless His holy name.
> Bless the Lord, O my soul,
> And forget none of His benefits. (Ps. 103:1–2)

It would be difficult for others not to notice such a perspective. An attitude of grateful joy, like the smile of a child, is contagious and one of the most convincing witnesses of the reality of Christ in our lives.

Earnest in Prayer

To discover the next factor, we follow Paul into the secret world of his prayer life.

> We night and day keep praying most earnestly that we may see your face, and may complete what is lacking in your faith. (1 Thess. 3:10)

He prayed "night and day," continually and fervently. Two specific requests were on his lips, the first of which was that he might see his friends again. Probably, he was praying that God would block Satan from cutting in on his plans to travel back to Thessalonica. How desperately he wished God would clear a path for him to return to them soon.

The reason for his desire is found in his second request: he wanted to "complete" what was lacking in their faith. Their loop of spiritual understanding was not yet closed, and he yearned to complete what was missing. The Greek word for *complete*, *katartizō*, has a varicolored meaning:

> To fit together, to join together, to restore, to repair, to equip. The word had a variety of usages depending upon the context. It was used to reconcile political factions. It was a surgical term for "setting bones." It was used for repairing nets (Mark 1:19). It was

used of making military and naval preparations.[2]

We can imagine Paul as a medical doctor, applying a healing balm of truth to the people's souls; as a fisherman, mending the broken threads in their doctrine; or as commander, equipping them to do battle with the Evil One. All this he longed to do for the Thessalonians . . . if the Father willed. He was dependent on the Lord for his future and for the future of the believers. Continually and earnestly through prayer, he was handing his burden for them into the hands of God.

Could it be that we don't "really live" because we try to carry the burdens that God should bear? God never designed prayer to add to our load but to help lighten it. Think of prayer not as another daily chore, but as a minute-by-minute opportunity to unload your cares so you can walk erect and free. Now that's really livin'!

Abounding in Love

Paul not only told the people he was praying for them, he also wrote down his prayer in the form of a pastoral benediction. Within this blessing is the third factor of a life that is real: abounding love.

> Now may our God and Father Himself and Jesus our Lord direct our way to you; and may the Lord cause you to increase and abound in love for one another, and for all men, just as we also do for you.
> (vv. 11–12)

Just as the love between a man and woman increases more and more from courtship to engagement to marriage, Paul prayed that the Thessalonians' love would grow—not only for each other, but "for all men." The word *for* is *eis* in Greek, which can mean "into." The roots of their love were to grow deeply into each other's souls and the souls of the nonbelievers within their reach. Only the Lord can inspire that kind of penetrating and far-reaching affection.

We use the word *love* so often and in so many contexts, it is sometimes difficult to know what real love is. Perhaps, using the letters in the word, we can identify its components.[3]

---

2. Fritz Rienecker, A Linguistic Key to the Greek New Testament, ed. Cleon L. Rogers, Jr. (Grand Rapids, Mich.: Zondervan Publishing House, Regency Reference Library, 1980), pp. 595–96.

3. The acrostic is adapted from Seeds of Greatness, by Denis Waitley (Old Tappan, N.J.: Fleming H. Revell Co., 1983), p. 134.

L— *Listen.* When we love others, we respect and accept them enough to graciously listen to what they say and feel.

O— *Overlook.* For most of us, the first thing we notice in others is their flaws. Accepting others in love, however, entails passing over their weaknesses so that we can affirm their strengths.

V— *Value.* How often we say we love someone yet make him or her feel inferior through put-downs and harsh words. Real love honors and esteems others, making them feel valuable and capable.

E— *Express.* Love is a verb—it acts, it gives, it demonstrates itself in tangible ways. The Greek writer Aristides once described to the Emperor Hadrian how the early Christians expressed their love:

> They love one another. They never fail to help widows; they save orphans from those who would hurt them. If they have something they give freely to the man who has nothing; if they see a stranger, they take him home, and are happy, as though he were a real brother. They don't consider themselves brothers in the usual sense, but brothers instead through the Spirit, in God.[4]

Established in Holiness

The first three factors in Paul's life all build toward the fourth, which involves personal holiness. He prays that the Lord will in-crease the people's love

> so that He may establish your hearts unblamable in holiness before our God and Father at the coming of our Lord Jesus with all His saints. (v. 13)

"Be established in holiness," Paul says. "Plant your feet firmly on the bedrock of God's moral standard." The world may chip away at God's standards and try to convince us that "anything goes" and "if it feels good, do it." But when Christ comes again, we won't be standing before a human judge but before God. His idea of right

---

4. Aristides, as quoted by Charles W. Colson in *Loving God* (Grand Rapids, Mich.: Zondervan Publishing House, 1987), p. 173.

and wrong will be the standard. "Therefore," as Peter exhorts us,

> gird your minds for action, keep sober in spirit, fix
> your hope completely on the grace to be brought to
> you at the revelation of Jesus Christ. As obedient
> children, do not be conformed to the former lusts
> which were yours in your ignorance, but like the
> Holy One who called you, be holy yourselves also
> in all your behavior; because it is written, "You shall
> be holy, for I am holy." (1 Pet. 1:13–16)

Without the Lord's holy example and Christ's gracious empowering through the Spirit and the church, real living would be impossible. Our battles with the enemy would result in hopeless defeats. And we would become lonely, battered soldiers. Mentally, emotionally, and spiritually, we would turn again to the substitutes for real living.

Thankfully, though, we don't have to settle for substitutes. We can have the real thing!

Learning from This, We Grow

The result of these four factors coming together in our lives is personal growth. Mentally, we'll grow wiser; emotionally, we'll grow stronger; spiritually, we'll grow purer. The substitutes of the world can't nourish us like that. Like the artificial flavorings in our processed foods, they have little nutritional value. What we need are the healthy nutrients—joyful gratitude, prayer, love, and holiness. Real food is what we need . . . food for real living.

Living Insights STUDY ONE

Have you noticed how grateful people become after a frightful brush with death? For instance, observe heart patients coming home from the hospital—watch how they pause to take in the sweep of the sky, to linger in the warm sunshine, to lovingly hold their spouse's hand. They had almost lost it all; now it is all so wonderful.

Why does it take a near-death experience to remind us of God's blessings in our lives? Perhaps, like the Israelites in the wilderness, we've become accustomed to His mannalike goodness around us. After a while, we begin yawning at His daily miracles, ignoring them and even complaining about them. Not until we wake up one morning to discover they're not there do we wish we had appreciated them more.

What are some of the mannalike miracles in your life? List some of the wonders you may be taking for granted.

_____

_____

_____

Are there some people in your life whose value you've skipped over? Who are they?

_____

_____

_____

Take away our houses, toys, and money—reduce our lives to the bare minimum—and it's the people we love who bring us the greatest joy. Take a moment to thank the Lord for them. Then write down some ways you can express your gratitude to them today.

_____

_____

_____

Living Insights
STUDY TWO

We're not really living until we learn how to love. The main character in George MacDonald's story "My Uncle Peter" learned how to love through a little street-sweeping beggar girl. Every year, the generous bachelor Uncle Peter would buy lavish Christmas presents for his nephews and nieces, yet he still felt empty. Just buying presents wasn't enough. "I wish I could be of real, unmistakable use to any one," he said one year. "But I fear I am not good enough to have that honor done me."

Burdened with these thoughts, he went for a walk on Christmas Day and passed a young girl sweeping the crossing. "What is your name?" he asked her. "Little Christmas," she said.

When she told him about her abusive aunt and pitiful circumstances, he yearned to adopt her and love her as his own daughter. At last, he was "of real, unmistakable use" to someone. His gift of love to Little Christmas was his finest Christmas present ever.[5]

Giving love can bring meaning into your life too.

According to 1 Timothy 1:5, love was the goal of Paul's ministry. What three character qualities in his life did he strive for in order to achieve that purpose?

1. _____

2. _____

3. _____

Has one of these qualities been lacking in your life, blocking your ability to love others? Which one? What can you do to free yourself to love?

_____

_____

_____

Who needs your love right now? In what ways can you be like Uncle Peter to this person?

_____

_____

_____

Little children, let us not love with word or with tongue,
but in deed and truth. (1 John 3:18)

---

5. George MacDonald, "My Uncle Peter," in *The Christmas Stories of George MacDonald* (Elgin, Ill.: David C. Cook Publishing Co., Chariot Classics, 1981), pp. 7–34.

Chapter 6

STRAIGHT TALK ABOUT MORAL PURITY

1 Thessalonians 4:1–8

*H*oliness. The word conjures up so many pictures in our minds, as John White mused in his book *The Fight*.

> Have you ever gone fishing in a polluted river and hauled out an old shoe, a tea kettle or a rusty can? I get a similar sort of catch if I cast as a bait the word *holiness* into the murky depths of my mind. To my dismay I come up with such associations as:
>
> thinness
> hollow-eyed gauntness
> beards
> sandals
> long robes
> stone cells
> no sex
> no jokes
> hair shirts
> frequent cold baths
> fasting
> hours of prayer
> wild rocky deserts
> getting up at 4 A.M.
> clean fingernails
> stained glass
> self-humiliation[1]

With these mental pictures, we tend to cloister holiness in the hushed chambers of monasteries and cathedrals, where saints, hooded monks, and mystics reside. God, however, wants to unlock the wooden doors and open the stained-glass windows of our thinking so His holiness can walk freely through every room of our lives.

---

1. John White, *The Fight* (Downers Grove, Ill.: InterVarsity Press, 1976), p. 179.

He longs for us to be holy as He is holy—yes, ordinary, garden-variety people like us (see 1 Pet. 1:15–16). Chuck Colson writes,

> Holiness is the everyday business of every Christian.
> It evidences itself in the decisions we make and the
> things we do, hour by hour, day by day.[2]

Every day God calls us to be beacons of purity so that hope will pierce through to those who are stumbling in the world's moral fog—a fog that seems to only get thicker with time.

The Fog: An Analysis of Today's Moral Scene

Surprisingly, the most cogent analysis of today's moral scene is provided by two ancient prophets from the Old Testament. The first is Habakkuk. In his day, surging clouds of immorality shrouded the Hebrew people, and he begged the Lord to roll them back with the clean winds of His salvation.

> How long, O Lord, will I call for help,
> And Thou wilt not hear?
> I cry out to Thee, "Violence!"
> Yet Thou dost not save.
> Why dost Thou make me see iniquity,
> And cause me to look on wickedness?
> Yes, destruction and violence are before me;
> Strife exists and contention arises.
> Therefore, the law is ignored
> And justice is never upheld.
> For the wicked surround the righteous;
> Therefore, justice comes out perverted.
> (Hab. 1:2–4)

His world could be ours, couldn't it? As he walked the streets, brutal violence tore at his heart and sent him screaming in anguish to the Lord. "Iniquity"—the Hebrew word encompasses sins such as lying, vanity, and idolatry—constantly crowded and jostled him. And "wickedness," which refers to oppression, robbery, and assault, bruised and battered his senses. Strife, contention, contempt for lawful order, the twisting of justice—every sin that pollutes our

---

2. Charles W. Colson, *Loving God* (Grand Rapids, Mich.: Zondervan Publishing House, A Judith Markham Book, 1983), p. 131.

world was choking his. So he cried out to the Lord, "Aren't You the Holy One? How can You sit back and do nothing about this unholy place?"

Habakkuk screamed; the prophet Jeremiah just sobbed.

> "Be warned, O Jerusalem,
> Lest I be alienated from you;
> Lest I make you a desolation,
> A land not inhabited." . . .
> To whom shall I speak and give warning,
> That they may hear?
> Behold, their ears are closed,
> And they cannot listen.
> Behold, the word of the Lord has become a
>   reproach to them;
> They have no delight in it. (Jer. 6:8, 10)

Years after Habakkuk's prophecy, Jeremiah was still warning of God's impending judgment. Pervasive sin had clouded the land; and the people, unable to clearly delineate the sharp edges of truth anymore, persistently hedged on God's standards and cut corners. As a result, their ears were deaf to His saving Word. Tragically, it had even become "a reproach to them." Holiness was not delightful to them any longer—they detested it.

People living in today's fog of immorality often respond the same way, don't they? When a holy lifestyle is advocated, many throw their hands in the air: "Aw, c'mon! Get real! That gloom-and-doom guilt talk is old-fashioned—no one believes that anymore. Keep up with the times!" Such disdain for holiness made Jeremiah churn inside. He yearned for God to put an end to the greed and deception he saw all around him.

> "For from the least of them even to the greatest
>   of them,
> Everyone is greedy for gain,
> And from the prophet even to the priest
> Everyone deals falsely.
> And they have healed the brokenness of My
>   people superficially,
> Saying, 'Peace, peace,'
> But there is no peace." (vv. 13–14)

Jeremiah's finale in this litany of sin is a powerful and telling indictment against the people.

> "Were they ashamed because of the abomination
> they have done?
> They were not even ashamed at all;
> They did not even know how to blush." (v. 15a)

Isn't that the ultimate consequence of living in a moral fog? We become so accustomed to the pollution that our eyes no longer tear up, our consciences no longer sting, and our faces no longer burn with shame.

Still, the media continues barraging us with images of immorality. P. A. Sorokin, former professor of sociology at Harvard, observes the extent of this relentless bombardment:

> There has been a growing preoccupation of our writers with the social sewers, . . . the bedroom of the prostitute, a cannery row brothel, a den of criminals, . . . a club of dishonest politicians, a street corner gang of teen-age delinquents, a hate-laden prison, a crime-ridden waterfront, the courtroom of a dishonest judge, the sex adventures of urbanized cavemen and rapists, the loves of adulterers and fornicators, of masochists, sadists, prostitutes, mistresses, playboys. Juicy loves, id, orgasms, and libidos are seductively prepared and served with all the trimmings.[3]

And nobody blushes.

Worse yet, some even smirk and make jokes about it. However, those who deal with the ruinous consequences of incest or adultery or pornography don't see the humor. How urgent is the need for us to clear away the moral fog of our day and allow God's truth to shine through.

The Truth: God's Timeless Counsel for Christians

The apostle Paul longed for that shining truth to radiate through the Thessalonian believers as he prayed that God would establish them "unblamable in holiness" (1 Thess. 3:13a). What it means to

---

3. P. A. Sorokin, as quoted by Billy Graham in *World Aflame* (New York, N.Y.: Pocket Books, 1965), p. 18.

be unblamable, specifically with regard to sexual holiness, is the subject of the next chapter, verses 1–8. In this passage, the Lord looks His people straight in the eye and lovingly yet firmly gives the facts concerning sexual purity.

In Your Walk, Excel!

> Finally then, brethren, we request and exhort you in the Lord Jesus, that, as you received from us instruction as to how you ought to walk and please God (just as you actually do walk), that you may excel still more. For you know what commandments we gave you by the authority of the Lord Jesus. (vv. 1–2)

In his zeal for helping them achieve the confident security of being "unblamable in holiness," Paul stokes the Thessalonians' own fire for God with sparks of his encouragement. "You're doing great!" Paul says, "But don't settle there. Watch any tendency toward laziness or mediocrity, and soar into the heights God has prepared for you. Go for it! Excel!"

Our loving Father, in His grace, has given us great gifts and purposes to strive for—not to frustrate us, but because He wants only the highest and the best for His children. And this lifestyle of excellence has as part of its outworking a high moral ground, as Paul shows in the next few verses.

In Your Morals, Abstain!

> For this is the will of God, your sanctification; that is, that you abstain from sexual immorality. (v. 3)

From this verse, there is no doubt concerning God's will for our lives in the area of sex. We don't have to pray about whether we should have an adulterous affair or be sexually active before marriage. God's will is clear: we are to abstain from any illicit sexual relationship.[4]

---

4. "Christians are to avoid and abstain from any and every form of sexual practice that lies outside the circle of God's revealed will, namely adultery, premarital and extramarital intercourse, homosexuality, and other perversions. The word *porneia*, translated 'sexual immorality,' is a broad one and includes all these practices." Thomas L. Constable, "1 Thessalonians," in *The Bible Knowledge Commentary*, New Testament ed., ed. John F. Walvoord and Roy B. Zuck (Wheaton, Ill.: Scripture Press Publications, Victor Books, 1983), p. 701. Based on Jesus' statement in Matthew 5:28, this would also include voyeurism and lust. See also Leviticus 18:1–23; 20:10–26.

In today's moral grayness, some would say that such a black-and-white standard seems fanatic. After all, in certain situations, if people love each other, are discreet, and use precautions—what's the harm? But Scripture does not merely say, "Be careful"; it says, "Abstain."

The child of God who wishes to excel in his or her walk with the Lord must take this command seriously. Living in purity not only gives glory to the God who created sex for the marriage relationship but also provides us a healthy sense of self-respect and well-being. Still, the world and our own flesh urge us to disregard God's holiness. What can we do to stay pure? Continuing on the subject of God's will for our lives, Paul offers us some practical measures:

> This is the will of God . . . that each of you know how to possess his own vessel in sanctification and honor, not in lustful passion, like the Gentiles who do not know God; and that no man transgress and defraud his brother in the matter because the Lord is the avenger in all these things, just as we also told you before and solemnly warned you. (vv. 3a, 4–6)

Abstaining begins with "possessing" our own vessels, that is, knowing our own bodies—how our sex drives function, what weakens our self-control, and what strengthens it. Possessing our bodies involves admitting the temptations we can't handle and avoiding those enticing situations. Certain conversations with coworkers may lure us, and friendly touches may be too personal—avoid those situations. Some films, books, or magazines may ignite lustful passions, and some settings may provide opportunities for compromise—stay away from them. No one remains pure by accident. Abstaining from immorality means aggressively building protective walls against lust long before we have the opportunity to become physically involved in fornication or adultery.

Positively, it means becoming involved in wholesome pursuits, finding friends who keep us accountable, and cultivating faith in the Spirit's inner power. It means standing up as Christians, not for the purpose of leading a flag-waving crusade for moral purity, but to help others see in us the hope and security Christ offers.

To some, these measures may seem prudish, but better to be overly safe than risk the devastation sexual immorality causes. In fact, notice Paul's words, "that no man transgress and defraud his *brother*" (v. 6a). Immorality, a term describing every type of ungodly sexual behavior, affects not just the participants but the family as well. The spouses, children, parents, and siblings are all singed by its selfish fire—particularly in the case of incest, which this verse may be referring to.

How careful are you with regard to your personal holiness? Is there a part of your life hidden in the shadows of sexual immorality? Keep in mind that there are no secrets before God, and He is "the avenger in all these things." Although in Christ we're protected from His eternal punishment, God may still allow the consequences of our sexual sin to discipline us now. Paul wrote to the Corinthians,

> Flee immorality. Every other sin that a man commits is outside the body, but the immoral man sins against his own body. (1 Cor. 6:18)

Immorality leads to anxiety, conflict, guilt, and even physical disease, not to mention the long-lasting emotional wounds experienced by innocent family members. This is the bitter harvest we reap from planting seeds of impurity, for, as the saying goes, when we

> sow a thought, we reap an act;
> sow an act, and we reap a habit;
> sow a habit, and we reap a character;
> sow a character, and we reap a destiny.

Only through God's power in Christ can we begin sowing the seeds of righteousness.

In Your Reasoning, Remember!

In the final two verses of this passage, two key thoughts remain that will help us sow the right kind of seeds. First, we must remember that we have been called to growth.

> For God has not called us for the purpose of impurity, but in *sanctification*. (1 Thess. 4:7, emphasis added)

This is the third time Paul has used this word in this passage. It refers to our spiritual pilgrimage from Adam's image to Christ's image. Sometimes our rate of growth is fast, sometimes slow, but always the goal of maturity in Christ motivates us to remain pure.

The second thought to remember is: to reject holiness is to reject God.

Consequently, he who rejects this is not rejecting man but the God who gives His Holy Spirit to you. (v. 8)

Sometimes we can be like Peter, saying we would never deny our Lord; yet, through our actions, we reject His holiness and His power. If we truly believe in a holy God, holy living will be our goal.

The Choice: A Decision Only You Can Make

So we are left with two options. The first is to live on the horizontal plane, floating through life in society's fog of moral uncertainties. Living like this, we would probably rationalize away any feelings of guilt and, when tempted, begin to experiment with immorality. Eventually, our consciences would dull, and our tears of remorse would no longer flow . . . we'd stop blushing.

The second option is to live on the vertical plane, drawing power from the Spirit and building walls of moral purity. As a result, there will be no regrets, no looking over our shoulders for past secrets to catch up to us. We would enjoy lives of honor and confidence before God.

Lord,
free us to live unblamable
in holiness. Give us the power
to be pure!

Living Insights   STUDY ONE

Frederick Buechner has penned perhaps the most accurate definition of lust ever written: "Lust is the craving for salt of a man who is dying of thirst."[5]

Isn't that true? Is there a "salt" you have been craving, possibly even tasting? Maybe it is the forbidden delights in the pages of romance novels. Or the airbrushed allure of pornography. Perhaps your salt comes in the form of intriguing fantasies played out on daytime TV. Maybe it is the heart-pounding passion of a secret

5. Frederick Buechner, *Wishful Thinking: A Theological ABC* (New York, N.Y.: Harper and Row, Publishers, 1973), p. 54.

51

rendezvous. It could be so intimate that we dare not ask you to write it down; it's too personal even for a diary.

In all of this, though, your deepening thirst reveals that you are only tasting salt. Where is the water that will quench your parched soul?

A certain woman standing beside a well once asked Jesus that same question. Take a few moments to read her story in John 4:1–26.

What do you think the woman was thirsting for in her relationships with men? Why do you suppose those relationships did not satisfy her thirst?

_____

_____

_____

_____

What might you be thirsting for through your cravings?

_____

_____

_____

Jesus promised the woman "living water" (v. 10). How would that have satisfied her thirst? And, likewise, how can that water fulfill the yearnings of your soul?

_____

_____

_____

Defeating the power of lust begins with a devoted, worshipful relationship with Jesus Christ. Unless we're being nourished by His living water, no amount of willpower can weaken our craving for salt. Do you truly wish to surrender yourself to Him? To please God even in the hidden chambers of your life? If so, commit in your heart right now to throw away the salt and drink at His well.

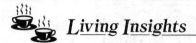

One wise person wrote,

> The good things on earth—food, drink, sex, recognition, power, wealth—are not spoiled; we are. They are relics of Eden. But our amnesia affects our very ability to determine their proper use.[6]

Has your sin nature's amnesia affected how you view your sexuality? Perhaps, bombarded by the world's lust-filled images, you've forgotten that sex is one of the "good things on earth"—a leftover from Paradise. If you have difficulty accepting your own sexuality and the goodness of its expression in marriage, read through God's inspired manual for marriage, The Song of Solomon. Then read Paul's comments in 1 Timothy 4:1–5. What do these Scriptures tell you about God's perspective concerning sex? What should our attitude be?

_____

_____

_____

_____

By respecting sex for what it is—of God's own design and good—you'll be more motivated to avoid society's cheap substitutes. The world will try to lure you to trade your sexual birthright for a bowl of pornography or a pot of adulterous fantasy or a kettle of singles'-bar excitement. Safeguard your gift. Respect its power. Cherish its beauty. And thank the Lord for your sexuality.[7]

---

6. "The War Within Continues" in _Leadership_ (Winter 1988), p. 32.

7. Some verses that may prove helpful in channeling your sexual urges for their proper use are Job 31:1; Romans 13:14; 1 Corinthians 6:18–20; and 2 Timothy 2:22. Also, please see the section at the end of this study guide, Books for Probing Further, for more specific resources on how to maintain your sexual purity in today's world.

Chapter 7

BEHAVING PROPERLY TOWARD OUTSIDERS

1 Thessalonians 4:9–12

D o you ever wonder how you, someone in Christ, are supposed to relate to those outside Christ? In attempting to formulate a plan, some Christians have fallen overboard into the high seas of extremes.

For example, some of us build our own little "Christian" world and have no contact with "outsiders." We speak our own Christian lingo with our own Christian friends, often in our own Christianly decorated homes. We listen to Christian radio, watch Christian TV, and play Christian music. We go to Christian barbers who give us Christian haircuts. We buy our gas from Christian station owners who pump Christian gas into our Christian cars . . . and on and on!

To avoid this extreme, others of us go the opposite direction and become undercover saints who expertly camouflage our faith. We don't risk offending others, but by blending in, we lose our distinctiveness as followers of Jesus.

Both of these approaches only distort Christ's message and dilute its impact. And no one knows this better than our enemy Satan. One of his favorite tactics is to tip our ship—ever so slightly—and watch us lose our solid footing and go plunging into extremes. Jesus, however, the Friend of sinners, offers us another option—one that protects us against extremes and helps us keep an even keel.

Necessary Warning to All Christians

Jesus revealed His plan of balance in a prayer the night before His crucifixion.

> "I am no more in the world; and yet they [His fol-
> lowers] are in the world, and I come to Thee. Holy
> Father, keep them in Thy name, the name which
> Thou hast given Me, that they may be one, even as
> We are. . . . Now I come to Thee; and these things
> I speak in the world, that they may have My joy
> made full in themselves. I have given them Thy
> word; and the world has hated them, because they

are not of the world, even as I am not of the world. *I do not ask Thee to take them out of the world, but to keep them from the evil one.* They are not of the world, even as I am not of the world. Sanctify them in the truth; Thy word is truth. As Thou didst send Me into the world, I also have sent them into the world." (John 17:11, 13–18, emphasis added)

Jesus could have prayed, "Father, the world has hated them because they are not of this world. So spare them the pain, and take them away from here." But instead, He wanted His followers to remain behind, and He only asked that the Father would protect them. It was as if He was saying, "Do not isolate them, Father, but insulate them." Why would He leave His followers here? So that, sanctified by the truth, we would bring light to those in the world's darkness. However, we're not to be so spiritual that we're out of this world. Therein lies the balance—being in the world but not of the world.

With this plan also comes a challenge: we must remain distinctive yet attractive to the world. The apostle Paul delineated this point for the Corinthians, who had isolated themselves from "sinners" while continuing to fellowship with an incestuous church member.

> I wrote you in my letter not to associate with immoral people; I did not at all mean with the immoral people of this world, or with the covetous and swindlers, or with idolaters; for then you would have to go out of the world. But actually, I wrote to you not to associate with any so-called brother if he should be an immoral person, or covetous, or an idolater, or a reviler, or a drunkard, or a swindler— not even to eat with such a one. For what have I to do with judging outsiders? Do you not judge those who are within the church? But those who are outside, God judges. Remove the wicked man from among yourselves. (1 Cor. 5:9–13)

Paul gives us a hard truth: we need to be tough on our own and easy on outsiders.[1] In fact, there will be rare occasions when we'll

---

1. For more information on the difficult task of church discipline, see John White's and Ken Blue's book *Church Discipline That Heals* (Downers Grove, Ill.: InterVarsity Press, 1985). (This book was formerly titled *Healing the Wounded*.)

need to exclude an unrepentant Christian while opening our arms to an unsaved person committing the very same sins.

Warmly receiving outsiders, though, is often the opposite of what we're told to do. New believers are usually advised to cut off their non-Christian relationships, until eventually, they have forgotten how to relate to outsiders. All the doors to the world have been shut tight.

Reopening those doors is a tough task for many of us. Put off by non-Christians' earthy lifestyles, we may either ignore them, hoping they'll go away, or we may try to scrub them clean so they'll fit in. And sometimes we're downright pleased when they're uncomfortable in our presence—"The Cross really offended today!" we'll beam, when, in fact, it was we who did the offending.

Jesus never made secular people feel uneasy around Him. The purest of the pure, He could lovingly look the sin-scarred prostitute in the eyes and welcome her with forgiveness. He could share a meal with a traitorous tax-collector and show him kindness. He could live in the world yet not be of the world, be attractive to others yet distinct. That is our greatest challenge.

The apostle Paul helps us understand more specifically how to meet that challenge in his words to the Thessalonian believers. In their zeal for Christ, these early Christians had been removing themselves from the world, giving outsiders a bad impression of Christianity. Let's follow Paul's train of thought as he offers them some balanced counsel.

Balanced Counsel from Early Christians

We might think that the Apostle would immediately encourage the Thessalonians to reestablish contact with the non-Christians around them. However, Paul focuses instead on what the world first notices about Christians—how they treat one another.

When It Comes to Fellow Christians

> Now as to the love of the brethren, you have no need for anyone to write to you, for you yourselves are taught by God to love one another; for indeed you do practice it toward all the brethren who are in all Macedonia. But we urge you, brethren, to excel still more. (1 Thess. 4:9–10)

Contagious Christianity is, above all else, loving Christianity. The Thessalonians had learned this directly from God's influence in their lives, and they had been practicing it not just among the believers in their own church but toward Christians throughout the region (see 1:2–3, 6–7). So as a coach addressing his team on a winning streak, Paul exhorts them, "Keep on going! You're doing great!"

Our model for this quality of love is Jesus. Notice how John described His love: "Having loved His own who were in the world, He loved them *to the end*" (John 13:1b, emphasis added). This phrase in Greek, *eis telos*, means more than "His love lasted for a long time." According to commentator A. W. Pink, it tells that Christ loved them "to the *farthest extent* of their need and His grace."[2]

That's the love in which Paul encourages the Thessalonians to excel. "Let your love have no limits," he urges them. Love others even when they don't deserve it, when they haven't met the conditions of a good love relationship. Love them enough to tell them the truth, enough to speak up when they're heading in harm's way.

This kind of unconditional, giving love is a spring of cool water to the parched souls of the unsaved. To them, love is often earned, so it never quite satisfies. Many times, a taste of Christian love is all that is needed to convince people of the gospel's truth (see John 13:34–35).

When It Comes to Non-Christians

Our love for fellow believers attracts the world in an indirect way. But Paul goes further to address how we should directly relate to non-Christians.

> Make it your ambition to lead a quiet life and attend
> to your own business and work with your hands, just
> as we commanded you; so that you may behave prop-
> erly toward outsiders and not be in any need.
> (1 Thess. 4:11–12)

When we think of impacting nonbelievers, we often picture overflowing crusades or people wearing "Ask Me about Jesus" buttons and handing out tracts. In this passage, though, Paul sees our influence coming in the nuts and bolts of our day-to-day lives. And he has four specific areas in mind.

---

2. Arthur W. Pink, *Exposition of the Gospel of John*, 3 vols. in 1 (Grand Rapids, Mich.: Zondervan Publishing House, 1975), vol. 2, p. 296.

First, *lead a quiet life*. This seems like a strange command; why would Paul paradoxically advise the Thessalonians to, as one commentator put it, "seek strenuously to be still"?[3]

The answer can be found by reading the rest of chapter 4, in which Paul addresses the Thessalonians' confusion about the Rapture. Hysteria regarding Christ's return had motivated some of them to quit their jobs so they could more fervently announce the end of the world.[4] Paul, however, wanted to channel that enthusiasm into "quiet" or ordinary living. They were still in the world, so they needed to do all the things that were necessary to live in the world: support their families, help the community, be a good neighbor, and so on.

Second, *attend to your own business*. Paul's word of advice to us is "Faithfully accomplish your assignments in life." For example, at work it can be so easy, because we're in love with Christ, to spend our time witnessing instead of getting the job done. We accomplish far more for Him by being dependable in our assignments, communicating Christ through our attitude, talking about Him when appropriate.

Third, *work with your hands*. With their end-times fervor telling them, What's the use in building something today, only to leave it behind tomorrow? the Thessalonian believers' lifestyle was degenerating into slack living and freeloading. This was such a severe problem that Paul had to admonish them with an even heavier hand in his second letter:

> For we hear that some among you are leading an undisciplined life, doing no work at all, but acting like busybodies. Now such persons we command and exhort in the Lord Jesus Christ to work in quiet fashion and eat their own bread. (2 Thess. 3:11–12)

When we can earn our own wage but refuse to do so, we forfeit the right to be heard regarding the Good News; an irresponsible, lazy lifestyle discredits the gospel. Someone once said that there are far too many people ready to carry the stool when there's a piano

---

3. Leon Morris, *The First and Second Epistles to the Thessalonians*, rev. ed., The New International Commentary on the New Testament series (Grand Rapids, Mich.: William B. Eerdmans Publishing Co., 1991), p. 131.

4. See Morris, *Epistles to the Thessalonians*, pp. 130–31.

to be moved! As those bearing Christ's name, we need to be among the first to lend a hand with the piano.

Fourth, *don't be overly dependent on others*. If we follow Paul's first three commands, we will usually "not be in any need" (1 Thess. 4:12). Of course, sometimes the bottom falls out of our lives and we do need a hand up. At those times, God has given us fellow believers and the church upon whom we can depend. The goal of our lives, however, is not to live off of others, but to be responsible and faithful with the strengths and abilities God has given us.

Practical Advice regarding Non-Christians

To wrap up our thoughts on our behavior toward those outside Christ, let's make three observations based on Paul's advice to the Colossian believers:

> Conduct yourselves with wisdom toward outsiders, making the most of the opportunity. Let your speech always be with grace, seasoned, as it were, with salt, so that you may know how you should respond to each person. (Col. 4:5–6)

They are watching and wondering, so conduct yourself with wisdom. Punctual arrival at work, willingness to take the difficult assignments, honesty about expenses—these are the things non-Christians notice long before we open our mouths about Christ. And these are the things that will help them become willing to listen.

They are listening and learning, so speak your words with grace. Are our words sprinkled with grace? Or are they harsh and demanding or perhaps loaded with secret codes and exclusiveness? Be aware of the words you use; let them be pleasing in their kindness and truth as well as seasoned with insight.

They are individuals and important, so respond with dignity and sensitivity. Did you catch the last phrase of Paul's advice—"that you may know how you should respond to *each person*" (emphasis added)? Sometimes it's easier to give people a canned presentation of the gospel rather than trying to tailor our words to their individual needs. The language of grace, though, is attentive and genuine. It's the language of Christ.

Paul used only two carefully chosen Greek words to write "make it your ambition to lead a quiet life" (1 Thess. 4:11a):

- *philotimeomai*, which means "to fix one's aim on, to strive earnestly for"[5]

- *hēsuchazō*, meaning "to be at rest, to be quiet, to remain silent"[6]

Literally, Paul said, "Strive to be quiet." This appears to be a contradiction in terms, doesn't it? How can we be striving and resting at the same time?

The answer is in our definition of "quiet" living. This is not a thumb-twiddling idleness; rather, it is a peace of mind, a complete freedom from anxious busyness. Certainly, that kind of lifestyle does not come automatically; we must make it our ambition.

Reflect on your life for a moment. If you could put a stethoscope up to your heart and its worries, what would you hear?

❑ A breeze rustling leaves in a lush green forest
❑ Thunder rumbling in the distance
❑ Workmen sawing wood and pounding nails
❑ The final screaming lap of the Indianapolis 500

With hearts pounding about the end of the world, some of the Thessalonians were frantically busying themselves in Christian activities. If you sense a panic in your life, what has invaded your quietness?

_____

_____

Paul's advice was to return to basics: "Attend to your own business and work with your hands" (v. 11b). What basics might you need to refocus on?

_____

_____

5. Morris, *Epistles to the Thessalonians*, p. 131.

6. Fritz Rienecker, *A Linguistic Key to the Greek New Testament*, ed. Cleon L. Rogers, Jr. (Grand Rapids, Mich.: Zondervan Publishing House, Regency Reference Library, 1980), p. 598.

What steps do you need to take to achieve quieter living?

_____

_____

_____

If we're overly busy, we rarely have time for outsiders; but a calm, peaceful spirit offers nonbelievers a genuine welcome. Won't you ask the Lord right now for that tranquility of mind only He can offer? Then, be ambitious . . . about being quiet.

Living Insights

According to Paul, diligence on the job is an important factor in making Christianity attractive to non-Christians. But what do we do when our jobs get us down—those days when our workload only gets heavier and our bosses just get more exasperating?

The Apostle helps us adjust our attitude with his words to the Colossian believers:

> Whatever you do, do your work heartily, as for the Lord rather than for men. (Col. 3:23)

Walter Wangerin offers us insight into Paul's words.

> If a carpenter crafts a chair for a rich stranger, he may do it well; but if he crafts it for his daughter, he will do it lovingly. Much, much is different between the first and the second crafting; and much is different between the two chairs, too, though only he and his daughter may see the difference.[7]

Christians who do their work for the Lord do it not only for the pay but for the gleam in Christ's eyes when we present it to Him. This week, do your work as a gift of love to the Lord. Your boss may not see the difference, but Christ will.

---

7. Walter Wangerin, Jr., *Measuring the Days*, ed. Gail McGrew Eifrig (San Francisco, Calif.: HarperSanFrancisco; Grand Rapids, Mich.: Zondervan Publishing House, 1993), p. 213.

Chapter 8

ON THAT GREAT GETTIN'-UP MORNING

1 Thessalonians 4:13–18

Down at a country store somewhere in the Deep South, a few raggedy young men had draped themselves over the front porch rail to sip cola and razz passersby, when up came an older woman, Miz Bessie—a fine, stout, Christian woman, nourished through the years by the Good Book, fried chicken, and sensible living. She stopped, sized up the smirking boys through her bifocals, and climbed the stairs to tend to her shopping.

"Preacher says Jesus comin' soon, Miz Bessie," called one fellow through grinning eyes.

"You b'lieve Jesus comin' soon, Miz Bessie?" taunted another, holding in a snicker like steam in the belly of a stove.

Flashing a glance at the lolling boys, she straightened her shoulders. "I do indeed; sure as you was born," she said.

They pressed her. "Well, ain't you better hurry home and get ready? Jesus might be on His way from glory right now!"

Having just stepped inside the store, she turned and stared into their mocking eyes. "Y'all listen here," she said slowly. "I don't have to get ready; I keeps ready!"

What a great answer! But it begs a penetrating question: Do you also "keeps" ready? Like Miz Bessie, are you living as if Jesus might any moment burst through heaven's door?

Perhaps, like the cynical boys in the story, you consider Christ's coming hard to accept. Or maybe you believe He is coming, but you're not quite as committed as the old woman. Thoughts of meeting Him face-to-face rarely find their way off the top shelf of your mind and into your daily experience.

In the New Testament, the subject of the Lord's return is very up-front, referred to over three hundred times—more than any other subject. It's even the final thought of Scripture: "Yes, I am coming quickly," He announces, and John responds, "Amen. Come, Lord Jesus" (Rev. 22:20). He could come again at any time, and He doesn't want us to forget it.

If we're not careful, though, we can take this awareness to

extremes, getting bogged down on miry side paths in our faith. Because we want you to keep to the high ground, let's spend a moment examining the pitfalls to watch out for.

Extremes We Need to Guard Against

One extreme is *fanatic intensity*, which is characterized by an over-reaction to Christ's return. Obsessed with end-times teaching, some people interpret every world event as a fulfillment of prophecy. A few even attempt to set the date of Christ's return and, in euphoric anticipation, quit their jobs and disregard their responsibilities. But always the date comes and goes, and they are left disillusioned.

The other extreme is *theological ignorance*. For some Christians, talk of God's prophetic timetable usually draws glassy stares and wide yawns. Unfortunately, this disinterest has a domino effect in their Christian life. Since they have little vision for the next world, they often lack passion for this world's lost and for their own personal purity. Death and the future terrify them, because they have not anchored themselves in the truth of Christ's glorious return.

A spin-off of this extreme is theological misinformation. Some people not only don't understand the truth, they believe what is untrue. This makes matters worse. As Mark Twain once quipped: "The trouble with the world is not that people know too little, but that they know so many things that ain't so."[1]

To help us know what is so and what "ain't so," let's examine Paul's words to the Thessalonian believers, who had veered into some swampy extremes of their own and needed to place their feet once again on truth's solid ground.

Truth We Can Count On

You'll recall from the previous chapter that the Thessalonian church was troubled by extremism. Ecstatic about Christ's imminent return, some people had quit their jobs and become freeloaders and busybodies. Also troubling the church was fear based on misinformation. The people were afraid that their Christian loved ones who had died before Christ's coming would be forgotten or somehow miss His return. So Paul builds for them and for us a firm theological

---

1. Mark Twain, in *Quote, Unquote*, comp. Lloyd Cory (Wheaton, Ill.: Scripture Press Publications, Victor Books, 1977), p. 172.

footing concerning death and the coming of Christ.

Regarding Our Death and Life Afterwards

Affirming the need for Christians to understand these truths, Paul begins:

> We do not want you to be uninformed, brethren, about those who are asleep. (1 Thess. 4:13a)

Asleep is a euphemism for death, minus the finality. It is a hopeful word, because sleeping assumes a future "awakening"—a resurrection. Motivating his words is his pastoral concern "that you may not grieve, as do the rest who have no hope" (v. 13b).

How tragic is the grief that has no hope. How desperate are the sobs of those left behind as they kneel beside the grave and try vainly to reach their dead. Relentless questions tear at their hearts: Where are they now? Are they in torment? Why go on living if this is our end?

Paul says we don't have to grieve like that. Notice, however, he doesn't say we're not to grieve. Don't let people tell you that strong Christians don't weep when death claims a loved one. The fact is, not until we experience the emotional depths of grief can we step into life's fullness again. We must "walk *through* the valley of the shadow of death" before we can reach the other side (Ps. 23:4a, emphasis added). But through that valley, God is by our side, reminding us of the eternal sunshine beyond the grieving and the grave.

The basis of our hope is that "Jesus died and rose again" (1 Thess. 4:14a)—the most significant statement in Scripture! Through His atoning sacrifice and His grave-defeating resurrection, Christ has conquered sin and death. As a result,

> if we believe that Jesus died and rose again, even so God will bring with Him those who have fallen asleep in Jesus. (v. 14)

There's that word again, *asleep*. As Paul unfolds the subject of our future resurrection, he makes it clear that God will arouse the "sleeping" bodies of dead believers. Paul's words to the Corinthians help round out our understanding of this event.

> Now I say this, brethren, that flesh and blood cannot inherit the kingdom of God; nor does the

perishable inherit the imperishable. Behold, I tell you a mystery; we shall not all sleep, but we shall all be changed. (1 Cor. 15:50–51)

Can you imagine keeping our aging, earthly bodies in heaven? After several million years, we wouldn't look so good, would we! We need new bodies to live in eternity—bodies not of perishable flesh and blood but of imperishable heavenly material. But how do we obtain them?

The answer is the "mystery" or the secret Paul is whispering in our ears—"Psst, we shall all be changed."[2] We may not all die before the time of the resurrection, but definitely, we will all be changed

> in a moment, in the twinkling of an eye, at the last trumpet; for the trumpet will sound, and the dead will be raised imperishable, and we shall be changed. For this perishable must put on the imperishable, and this mortal must put on immortality. (vv. 52–53)

In the instant it takes to see the sparkle in an eye, our bodies will be changed. What will they be like? Like Jesus' resurrection body—unrestricted by time, space, or matter (see John 20:19; 1 John 3:2b).

At that moment,

> when this perishable will have put on the imperishable, and this mortal will have put on immortality, then will come about the saying that is written, "Death is swallowed up in victory. O death where is your victory? O death, where is your sting?" (1 Cor. 15:54–55)

Finally, death will close its mouth and never again open its voracious jaws.

Regarding Christ's Coming and Others' Joining

With these strong truths in hand, let's return to 1 Thessalonians, where Paul lays out the order of events at Christ's dramatic appearing:

> For this we say to you by the word of the Lord, that

2. The Greek word for *mystery*, *musteriōn*, does not imply something confusing and complicated, like the intrigue of a mystery novel. Rather, it means "secret"—something hidden but simple to understand once told.

we who are alive, and remain until the coming of the Lord, shall not precede those who have fallen asleep. For the Lord Himself will descend from heaven with a shout, with the voice of the arch-angel, and with the trumpet of God; and the dead in Christ shall rise first. Then we who are alive and remain shall be caught up together with them in the clouds to meet the Lord in the air, and thus we shall always be with the Lord. (4:15–17)

Let's break down the events into an easy-to-follow timetable:

1. Christ Himself will descend from heaven.

2. There will be a shout, with the voice of the archangel and the trumpet of God.

3. The dead in Christ will rise first.

4. The living believers will join them in meeting the Lord in the air.

So, you see, we have nothing to fear concerning our loved ones who have died in Christ. They will be the first Christ gathers to Himself.

And what a family reunion that will be! Husbands and wives, parents and children, friends and relatives separated by death will join hands once again to live forever, together with Christ!

Regarding Confidence and Comfort

Therefore comfort one another with these words. (v. 18)

Paul's words are for the fearful, who wonder if Christ has for-gotten the dead; for the unsure, who consider eternity beyond their grasp; and for the grieving, who think the last rose on the coffin must be their final good-bye. Christ has not forgotten, eternal life is free, and death is only sleep. These are words of confidence and hope.

In Response to Christ's Soon Coming: What's Appropriate?

In light of all that we've learned, we must ask ourselves, "What does it mean to prepare for Christ's coming? How do I respond to this appropriately?" Paul provides direction in a letter to his friend Titus.

For the grace of God has appeared, bringing salvation to all men, instructing us to deny ungodliness and worldly desires and to live sensibly, righteously and godly in the present age, looking for the blessed hope and the appearing of the glory of our great God and Savior, Christ Jesus. (Titus 2:11–13)

First, *make certain you have taken what God has given—His salvation.* Christ died to pay for sins and rose to give you eternity. To be forgiven and to receive life, He asks simply that you place your belief in Him. Have you?

Second, *continue to resist a corrupt lifestyle.* Paul instructs us to "deny ungodliness and worldly desires" so we won't be caught unprepared. Are you?

Third, *live in a sensible, godly manner.* Live as if Christ might come today. Stay involved in Christ's program; give yourself to the Savior; share His love with others. Do you?

One day there will be a morning like no other. With a thundering shout and the blast of a trumpet, Christ will split the skies, graves will crack open, and we will all see Jesus. In the words of the old spiritual, that will be a "great gettin'-up morning"! Are you gettin' ready?

Better still, are you keepin' ready?

Living Insights

How do we "keeps" ready for the coming of the Lord? Let's look through the telescope of Scripture to discover some ways to keep our focus heavenward. According to the following verses, what benefits await Christians at the Lord's coming?

John 14:2–3 _____

2 Corinthians 5:1–5 _____

1 Peter 1:3–5 _____

What should be our attitude toward Christ's coming?

Mark 13:33–37 _____

Philippians 3:20 _____

2 Timothy 4:8b _____

What kinds of behaviors characterize those who are keeping ready?

Romans 13:11–14 _____

Philippians 4:5 _____

James 5:8–9 _____

1 Peter 4:7–11 _____

Suppose Christ told you that He was planning to come at midnight tomorrow. In what ways would that knowledge affect your perspective of God?

_____

_____

_____

In what ways would it affect how you relate to others?

_____

_____

_____

In what ways would it affect how you think about yourself?

_____

_____

_____

Christ may come at midnight tomorrow. Then again, He may come before you finish reading this sentence. What changes do you need to make to get ready? What must happen so you can keep ready?

_____

_____

_____

_____

On the tombstone of a husband and wife buried side by side, an epitaph reads:

> *Amavimus. Amamus. Amabimus.* ("We have loved. We love. We shall love.")[3]

Somehow, beyond the misty barrier of death, a reunion of lovers and friends awaits. For the Christian, that is not a romantic wish but a guarantee from the Lord Himself. Based on the following verses, write down the assurances God gives that you will be with your Christian loved ones for eternity.

2 Corinthians 4:13–15 _____

1 Thessalonians 2:19–20 _____

1 Thessalonians 4:17 _____

These words are pillows of comfort upon which we can rest our fears. Do you fear death's separation from a spouse or loved one? Are you right now grieving a loss? In the space provided, express those fears and sorrows. What comfort do you feel in knowing you will one day meet your loved ones again?

_____

_____

_____

_____

_____

You have loved. You love. You shall love. "Therefore comfort one another with these words" (1 Thess. 4:18).

---

3. Carroll E. Simcox, comp., *4400 Quotations for Christian Communicators* (Grand Rapids, Mich.: Baker Book House, 1991), p. 118.

Chapter 9

"... LIKE A THIEF IN THE NIGHT"

1 Thessalonians 5:1–11

Within each of us is an insatiable curiosity to know the future. What will happen to the economy? Will our children grow up healthy and stable? Will my job prove to be all I hoped it would be? Oh, to be able to pull back the curtain of time and peek into tomorrow's mysteries!

Because that curiosity is so powerful, we are often drawn to prophecy passages like the ones in 1 Thessalonians. And we are intrigued by modern-day prophets who link current events with Scripture and cry out with conviction, "Behold, the future!"

If we're not careful, though, our curiosity can get us into trouble. Some prophecy "experts" bait people with sensational predictions that have little basis in Scripture. Of course, these false prophets eventually reveal their true identity when their seerlike powers fail them—like the psychic who placed the following notice in a local paper:

> Due to unforeseen circumstances, no Clairvoyant meeting tonight, until further notice.[1]

That "prophet" wouldn't have much luck getting people to show up for the next meeting! So when it comes to future things, we must proceed carefully, claiming only what Scripture claims and being aware of a few facts concerning the subject of prophecy.

The Subject of Prophecy

Initially, it is important to understand that our curiosity about prophecy and the future is God-given. According to Solomon, the Lord has placed eternity in our hearts—He has created us with a hunger that only His truth can satisfy (Eccles. 3:11a). We observe that craving, for instance, in the disciples' request of Jesus:

> "Tell us, when will these things be, and what will

---

1. *Lockport, N.Y., Union-Sun and Journal,* as quoted in *Quote Unquote,* comp. Lloyd Cory (Wheaton, Ill.: Scripture Press Publications, Victor Books, 1977), p. 263.

be the sign of Your coming, and of the end of the age?" (Matt. 24:3b)

Even though we have eternity in our hearts, many aspects of God's truth remain a mystery (Eccles. 3:11b). God's complete plan for the ages is always just beyond our reach. That is why Jesus later responded to His disciples:

"It is not for you to know times or epochs which the Father has fixed by His own authority." (Acts 1:7)

We are in danger when we begin speculating about aspects of prophecy that are supposed to be unclear. God doesn't want us to know every detail about the "times or epochs," so we have no business setting dates or detailing events for them. Perhaps the following motto would serve as a helpful warning: Those who leave little room for mystery leave lots of room for mistakes.

So, as we balance our curiosity with the reality of mystery, let's examine a fascinating yet sobering portion of prophecy in 1 Thessalonians 5:1–11.

The Day of the Lord

In 1 Thessalonians 4, Paul comforted the believers who feared that their dead loved ones would miss Jesus' return. At any moment, he assured them, "The Lord Himself will descend from heaven" and gather up His followers to Himself, both the living and the dead (vv. 16–17). We refer to this glorious reunion as the Rapture of the church.

In chapter 5, the Apostle continues comforting his readers, who, because of their hardships, also feared that the terrible Day of the Lord had begun (see 2 Thess. 2:1–2).[2] This period of God's judgment, entailing horrible, inescapable affliction, will follow the Rapture and is known as the Tribulation.[3] Paul tells them, "Don't worry!

2. According to Scripture, the Day of the Lord will be filled with pestilence, natural disasters, and wars, culminating in the Second Coming of Christ and the Battle of Armageddon (see Joel 2:1–11; Rev. 16:12–16; 19:11–21).

3. In our study, we will be presenting the pretribulational view of the Rapture, which maintains that the church will be taken up with Christ before God releases His Tribulation wrath. However, many qualified scholars teach that the church may have to go through half or all of the Tribulation—the midtribulation or the post-tribulation view. For a discussion of all three positions, see *The Rapture: Pre-, Mid-, or Post-Tribulational?* by Richard R. Reiter, Paul D. Feinberg, Gleason L. Archer, and Douglas J. Moo (Grand Rapids, Mich.: Zondervan Publishing House, Academie Books, 1984).

The Day of the Lord is coming, but it concerns unbelievers, not believers."

The Coming of the Day

> Now as to the times and the epochs, brethren,
> you have no need of anything to be written to you.
> For you yourselves know full well that the day of
> the Lord will come just like a thief in the night.
> (1 Thess. 5:1–2)

The Apostle didn't need to tell them anything more by letter than what he had already taught them in Thessalonica; namely, that the Day of the Lord would come silently and suddenly—"like a thief in the night." But notice a distinction between this dreaded event and the grand appearing of Christ, who will

> descend from heaven with a shout, with the voice of
> the archangel, and with the trumpet of God. (4:16a)

Not too many thieves announce their arrival by shouting, "Here I come!" while being accompanied by singing voices and blaring trumpets. The Day of the Lord must be something altogether different than the Rapture—and not just because of how it comes but because of who it affects.

Unbelievers and the Day

> While they are saying, "Peace and safety!" then de-
> struction will come upon them suddenly like birth
> pangs upon a woman with child; and they shall not
> escape. (5:3)

Shifting the pronouns from "you" to "they," Paul now refers to unbelievers who remain on earth after the Rapture. Glad that the Christian influence is finally gone, they will follow the Antichrist and his scheme to rule the world (see Rev. 13:1–10). Their banners and slogans will enthusiastically portray the dawning of a new day of "peace and safety." Then, with swift terror, destruction will come.

In the earthquake-prone areas of California, scientists have long been warning people that a shaker of devastating magnitude is coming. Even so, not many Californians are adequately prepared for such a catastrophe. "Peace and safety," they say with a yawn.

In that same way, as commentator Robert Thomas describes,

unbelievers in the Tribulation will be

> priding themselves on their secure life styles. "Peace" characterizes their inward repose, while "safety" reveals their freedom from outward interference. . . . Yet at the moment that tranquility seemingly reaches its peak, "destruction will come on them suddenly." "Destruction" means utter and hopeless ruin, a loss of everything worthwhile . . . , causing the victims to despair of life itself (Rev 9:6). Without being totally annihilated, they are assigned to wrath.[4]

To accent the abruptness and pain of God's wrath, Paul goes on to use the analogy of "birth pangs upon a woman with child." No pregnant woman knows exactly when her labor will begin. She may suddenly be jolted out of her sleep by sharp pains, her muscles powerfully and involuntarily constricting with increasing intensity as she nears the climax of birth. Likewise, sudden pain will come upon those in the Tribulation, and they will not be able to escape its climax of destruction.

Believers and the Day

"But you, brethren," Paul begins the next verse, shifting his focus back to believers. After the terrifying predictions of verses 2–3, the contrasting word "but" is a welcome relief.

> But you, brethren, are not in darkness, that the day should overtake you like a thief; for you are all sons of light and sons of day. We are not of night nor of darkness. (1 Thess. 5:4–5)

With this relief also comes responsibility:

> So then let us not sleep as others do, but let us be alert and sober. For those who sleep do their sleeping at night, and those who get drunk get drunk at night. But since we are of the day, let us be sober, having put on the breastplate of faith and love, and as a helmet, the hope of salvation. (vv. 6–8)

---

4. Robert L. Thomas, "1 Thessalonians," in *The Expositor's Bible Commentary*, ed. Frank E. Gaebelein (Grand Rapids, Mich.: Zondervan Publishing House, Regency Reference Library, 1978), vol. 11, p. 282.

Because unbelievers live in the darkness of spiritual ignorance, they are unaware of the disaster that awaits them. It is as if they are asleep or drunk or both. Even loud sirens and warning bells do not arouse them to the fact that their world is on fire.

But Christians live in the light of truth (see also John 3:19–21). Judgment is coming, and the way of escape is the Cross and the empty tomb. So Paul exhorts us, "Don't become spiritually dull and sleepy; stay alert." Like a sentry who listens in the night for any breaking twig that may betray a coming attack, we are to keenly watch for the signs of the Lord's coming and forewarn those around us.

Paul also urges us to keep "sober"; we mustn't numb our senses through drugs or laziness. We must be vigilant and keep our sentry armor on—the "breastplate of faith and love" and the "helmet" of salvation's hope—because our life-saving information is the world's only chance of rescue.

But that's not the only reason Paul tells us of the future.

> For God has not destined us for wrath, but for obtaining salvation through our Lord Jesus Christ, who died for us, that whether we are awake or asleep, we may live together with Him. Therefore encourage one another, and build up one another, just as you also are doing. (1 Thess. 5:9–11)

The Apostle does not conclude his instructions with a panicked warning: "The Tribulation is coming, so prepare yourselves for famines and wars." Instead, he says, "Relax. Don't worry. We're protected from God's Tribulation wrath." What greater encouragement could we share! Which is exactly Paul's practical point: we need to be encouraging, building up, and strengthening each other in Christ now. Are you?

The Issue of Urgency

Even as you read this, governments are collapsing and new powers are forming almost daily. Who would have imagined the collapse of Communism? The upheaval and despair in seemingly stable countries? The openness to new world orders? Like a master strategist, God appears to be maneuvering nations into place, like game pieces, for His final play.

In light of this urgency, we offer two pieces of counsel. First, to Christians, *don't be indifferent because tomorrow is secure.* There is work to be done today. Our knowledge of prophecy must produce in us a desire to live for Christ and a passion to rouse the sleeping unsaved.

And second, to the non-Christian, *don't be fooled because today seems calm.* The Scripture is clear—there is a storm coming tomorrow. And there is no escape without Christ.

Perhaps an illustration will help you understand the urgency of the hour. Many years ago, a Long Island man ordered an extremely sensitive barometer from a respected company, Abercrombie and Fitch.

> When the instrument arrived at his home he was disappointed to discover that the indicating needle appeared to be stuck pointing to the sector marked "Hurricane." After shaking the barometer vigorously several times—never a good idea with a sensitive mechanism—the new owner wrote a scathing letter to the store and, on the following morning, on the way to his office in New York, mailed it. That evening he returned to Long Island to find not only the barometer missing but his house as well! The needle of the instrument had been pointed correctly. There was a hurricane. The month was September, 1938.[5]

Today you may be on easy street. Your health is good, your bank account is growing, and you're enjoying life. But the needle is pointing to "Hurricane," and there's a storm coming. Will it come tomorrow? Perhaps. Do you really want to wait to find out? Trust Christ for your salvation today.

Living Insights

As long as the Day of the Lord remains a vague eventuality, our salvation hope will be as useful to us as a wool blanket on a balmy summer day. Only by feeling a blast of arctic wind from God's Tribulation winter will we appreciate hope's value and snuggle in its warmth.

---

5. E. Schuyler English, "The Church and the Tribulation," in *Prophetic Truth Unfolding Today,* ed. Charles Lee Feinberg (Westwood, N.J.: Fleming H. Revell Co., 1968), p. 32.

So, in the following verses, let's explore the icy prophecies concerning the Day of the Lord. Use the space provided to jot down some of the judgments God has in store for the world, and brace yourself for the cold.

Joel 2:1–11 _____

_____

Zephaniah 1:14–18 _____

_____

Revelation 6:7–17 _____

_____

Revelation 8:6–12 _____

_____

Revelation 16:1–9 _____

_____

Such dark, chilling prophecies. Is there any hope for us? Yes!

For God has not destined us for wrath, but for ob-
taining salvation through our Lord Jesus Christ, who
died for us, that whether we are awake or asleep, we
may live together with Him. (1 Thess. 5:9–10)

Such a warm, comforting promise! Take a few moments to express your gratitude to the Lord for His salvation, then wrap yourself in His hope whenever fears of the future swirl around your heart.

_____

_____

_____

_____

_____

_____

_____

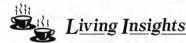

Those who live in the dark usually dream of power and profit, pleasure and happiness. But enough is never enough, and death always gets the final laugh. Solomon commented on the futility of it all:

> As he had come naked from his mother's womb, so will he return as he came. He will take nothing from the fruit of his labor that he can carry in his hand. And this also is a grievous evil—exactly as a man is born, thus will he die. So, what is the advantage to him who toils for the wind? (Eccles. 5:15–16)

Unbearable hopelessness. Drunkenness. Sleep. Escape. That's life in the darkness.

> But you, brethren, are not in darkness, . . . for you are all sons of light and sons of day. (1 Thess. 5:4a, 5a)

As a child of light, what is the hope God has given you (see 1 Pet. 1:3–5)?

_____

_____

In what ways does Christ want this hope to affect your lifestyle?

Romans 15:13 _____

Titus 2:11–13 _____

1 John 3:1–3 _____

Have you been living as those in the dark, placing your hope on earthly things? Has that hope disappointed you? Have you been finding solace by escaping? If so, how?

_____

_____

Today, refocus your dreams. Keep alert and sober. Live free from fear. You can be sure that Christ's hope "does not disappoint" (Rom. 5:5a). For it is "an anchor of the soul, a hope both sure and steadfast" (Heb. 6:19a).

Chapter 10

GIFTS TO GIVE THE FAMILY
1 Thessalonians 5:12–15

Christmas is the season of giving—perhaps that's why we love it so much. Surfacing from deep within us is a delightful spirit of unselfishness that makes the Christmas colors brighter and the music cheerier. We all seem to be in the giving mood as people crowd the stores buying things not for themselves but for others. Generosity decks the halls, gladdening everyone's hearts.

What are the best gifts we can give at Christmastime? The ones that show the depth of our love: gifts that last, that lift up the person receiving them, that cost us something—cause us to sacrifice ourselves in some way—and that give glory to God.

Paul provides us with a shopping list of these quality gifts in our Scripture passage—gifts not just for our immediate family but for the larger family of God as well. Although we can't buy these and wrap them in paper and ribbon, we can offer them wrapped in our own flesh and blood, and at any time, not just at Christmas. Let's peruse the items on the list one by one as Paul describes them in 1 Thessalonians 5.[1]

A God-Given Checklist to Follow

None of the gifts on this list are useless or trivial, like Day-Glo neckties or inside-the-egg eggbeaters. Each of them is essential for healthy relationships in the family of God and is just what our churches need today.

Paul begins, "We request of you" (v. 12), then later writes, "we urge you" (v. 14). These phrases form a natural division of the items in verses 12–15: things kindly requested and things urgently needed.

Things Kindly Requested

The first item on Paul's list is a gift we can give to our spiritual leaders.

---

1. Because the list is long, we'll cover the first half now and save the rest for the next chapter.

1. *Respect for those in leadership.* "We request of you, brethren," Paul begins,

> that you appreciate those who diligently labor among you, and have charge over you in the Lord and give you instruction, and that you esteem them very highly in love because of their work. (vv. 12–13a)

With three broad brush strokes, Paul portrays spiritual leaders as those who "diligently labor among you," "have charge over you in the Lord," and "give you instruction." These leaders could be men or women, lay or clergy, older or younger people—anyone who guides us in our spiritual walk.

We are to show them respect in two ways: "appreciate" them and "esteem them very highly in love." The Greek word translated *appreciate* is from the root verb *oida*, which simply means "to know." However, according to commentator Leon Morris, the word in this context

> has the idea of knowing fully, appreciating their true worth. It indicates that the brothers had not realized as they should have the rightful position and worth of the people in question, and they are called on to know them better.[2]

The other way we give respect is by esteeming our leaders. Paul is not saying that we should place them on a pedestal and blind ourselves to their faults. But neither should we hold back our praise, as some do, in an effort to keep them humble. To esteem our leaders is to acknowledge them, saluting their high calling and their hard work on our behalf.[3] Sadly, many leaders feel pistol-whipped by criticism, their slumped shoulders a testimony to having been treated with disrespect. How vital is this gift of honor to discouraged leaders!

2. *Live in peace with one another* (v. 13b). Paul's second request almost sounds cliché, doesn't it? The words may not have the sparkle of a diamond pendant, but they are just as precious. To produce

2. Leon Morris, *The First and Second Epistles to the Thessalonians*, rev. ed., The New International Commentary on the New Testament series (Grand Rapids, Mich.: William B. Eerdmans Publishing Co., 1991), p. 165.

3. Esteem for leaders is "because of their work" in the ministry, not necessarily their titles, degrees, or standing in the community. Leaders without formal training who devote themselves to their people and the Word ought to receive the same respect as seminary graduates.

such a gem in the family of God, we must quarry it in all our relationships with the diligence Paul describes in his letter to the Romans:

> Be devoted to one another in brotherly love; give preference to one another in honor; not lagging behind in diligence, fervent in spirit, serving the Lord; rejoicing in hope, persevering in tribulation, devoted to prayer, contributing to the needs of the saints, practicing hospitality. . . . Be of the same mind toward one another. . . . If possible, so far as it depends on you, be at peace with all men. (Rom. 12:10–13, 16a, 18)

"If possible"—the implication is that we can mine a relationship with such tools as love, honor, and hospitality and still discover no peace with the other person. So, because life is too short to spend it on fretting over the one who refuses to make peace, we should do all we can yet not feel responsible if the other person turns away.

Things Urgently Needed

Stepping up the intensity, Paul now says, "And we urge you, brethren" (1 Thess. 5:14a), and five more crucial gifts flow from Paul's pen.

1. *Admonish the unruly* (v. 14). Paul's first command in this category seems like an unusual gift. *Admonish* is a strong term that means to confront or call someone into account. It means to tell a person the truth in love, even though it may be difficult for him or her to face.[4]

The Apostle chooses a unique term to describe the "unruly"—*ataktos*. The only other occurrence of this word in the New Testament is in Paul's second letter to the Thessalonians. There it is translated as both "unruly" and "undisciplined."

> Keep aloof from every brother who leads an unruly life and not according to the tradition which you received from us. For . . . we did not act in an

---

4. By directing his comments to the "brethren" (vv. 12a and 14a), Paul limits this counsel to believers only. We must be careful not to admonish those outside the family of God for their behavior. They first need the power of Christ in their lives before they can begin cleaning up their lifestyles.

undisciplined manner among you. . . . For we hear that some among you are leading an undisciplined life, doing no work at all, but acting like busybodies. (2 Thess. 3:6b–7, 11)

According to Morris, the word was a military term that "originally referred to the soldier who is out of step or out of rank, or to the army moving in disarray."[5] Apparently, some of the Thessalonians had abandoned their posts and were continually neglecting their responsibilities. Relationships were immobilized and the church's witness was undermined because they would not change. Paul's command to them, and to us today, is to confront these believers and restore order in the ranks.

2. *Encourage the fainthearted* (1 Thess. 5:14). These dear people struggle under the weight of life's problems, often emotionally and physically drained by worry and fear. Do you know anyone who is fainthearted? "Give them the priceless gift of encouragement," says Paul.

This gift may be wrapped in an affirming word, a gentle touch, a smile, or a shoulder to lean on. It may simply be our presence. Too often we isolate ourselves; like strangers in an elevator, we feel uncomfortable even making eye contact or speaking politely to one another. In the family of God, though, things must be different. Let's free ourselves to touch one another, particularly the fainthearted, who need to know someone cares.

3. *Help the weak* (v. 14). The "weak" are the exhausted and burned-out ones, who may not even have the strength to handle their daily loads. When Paul tells us to help them, according to Morris, he is speaking of

> holding on to someone (e.g., Luke 16:13). The thought is that it is good for weak souls to know that there are others who are with them, who will cleave to them in the difficult moment, who will not forsake them.[6]

David had Jonathan to hold him up, Elijah had Elisha, and Paul had Epaphroditus, Epaphras, Luke, and Onesiphorus, to name a few. Some of these helpers we know well; others—we have trouble even spelling their names. Yet how could Paul have endured his imprisonments without friends like Onesiphorus, who, the Apostle said, "often

5. Morris, *Thessalonians*, p. 168.
6. Morris, *Thessalonians*, p. 169.

refreshed me, and was not ashamed of my chains" (2 Tim. 1:16b)?

To all the helpers in the family of God, thank you for cleaving to those who are weak through the long process of healing.

4. *Be patient with all* (1 Thess. 5:14). The Apostle adds the gift of patience to his list as a separate item, but it is a quality woven into the fabric of all the gifts. His word for *be patient* is *makrothumeō*, which literally means "long-tempered." It connotes the idea of having a long fuse, of not blowing up when others fail or change slowly. When we're patient, we don't brew with unforgiving irritability or restless anger. Rather, we are calm and long-suffering—we give ourselves and others, including those outside the family of God, time and space to grow.

5. *Refuse to retaliate.* The final gift we'll look at in 1 Thessalonians 5 is displayed in verse 15:

> See that no one repays another with evil for evil,
> but always seek after that which is good for one
> another and for all men.

Want to make this more personal? Insert into this verse your name and the name of your enemy—that is, anyone who has offended you or done you wrong: "See that *(your name)* does not repay *(your enemy)* with evil for evil, but always seek after that which is good for *(your enemy)* and for all men."

Not an easy verse to apply, is it? Perhaps the first half you can manage with some effort—not repaying evil for evil, harsh word for harsh word, fist for fist—but going the next step and offering goodness to an enemy seems impossible. Think of the revival, though, that would take place in the church if this gift were circulating in the family. Estranged friends would embrace one another again; brothers or sisters who haven't talked to each other for years would come together in love. What unity and love there would be!

Now imagine the worldwide revolution that would occur if this gift were given to "all men," as Paul concludes. Neighbors would take down their high fences; coworkers would help one another up the ladder of success. Even wars would cease as people sought the other's good instead of their own selfish desires.

Resources and Reminders

That's quite a gift list—and we're only halfway through! Before continuing in the next chapter, let's ask ourselves an important question: Where can we find what it takes to give these gifts? We have three resources. First, *we have in God's Word all the truth we'll ever need.* So read it to determine your correct path. Second, *we have in God's Spirit all the power we'll need.* So rely on Him for the strength to forgive, to be patient, and to encourage others. And third, *we have in God's family all the challenge we'll need.* In the family, we have people of every type and maturity level to relate to. Some who are similar to us will help us see ourselves for who we really are, and others who are different can broaden our thinking.

One last reminder: the church is not an edifice, an architectural dream, a place to impress the public. The church is a family of people in whom Christ reveals Himself. In order to experience the joy of giving, what can you offer the family of God? You have the shopping list before you; start with number one!

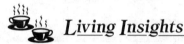 *Living Insights*   STUDY ONE

Let's spend some time bringing the gifts from our lesson to life. Consider each one very personally and practically.

1. *Respect for those in leadership.* Who are your spiritual leaders? Are you fully aware of their worth? List some of the things they do for you; then think of how you can show your esteem for them.

_____

_____

_____

2. *Live in peace with each other.* Do your words promote peace? Or do they produce strife by being accusatory, gossipy, or manipulative? What can you do to soften your approach?

_____

_____

_____

3. *Admonish the unruly.* Do you have a Christian friend or relative who has stepped out of line and is hurting Christ's family? What can you do to help guide him or her back into the ranks?

_____

_____

_____

4. *Encourage the fainthearted.* Who in your circle of acquaintances is overly burdened? How can you encourage them this week?

_____

_____

_____

5. *Help the weak.* You will not have to travel far to find the weak. Name one or two people who are crumbling under life's load. How can you hold them up?

_____

_____

_____

6. *Be patient with one another.* Have you had a long or short fuse this week? Have you wounded someone near you lately with an explosion of impatient anger? How can you heal that wound and give the gift of patience?

_____

_____

_____

7. *Refuse to retaliate.* "I'm going to give him a taste of his own medicine!" Or, "Let's see how she likes it when I treat her like she's been treating me!" Have these thoughts entered your mind recently? If so, using Christ as an example, how will you return good for evil or a smile for a frown in this relationship?

_____

_____

_____

Give some of these gifts to your own family today. Then reach out to those in the family of God, then to the world around you. The Christmas joy of giving can be yours all year long.

☕ *Living Insights* STUDY TWO

Suppose you have a Christian friend who has left God's path to walk in the ways of the world. No longer attending church, this person is closing off to spiritual things and neglecting family responsibilities. Your initial thought is: *I should admonish my friend.* Yet, when you meet with this person, you hear a story of heartache, frustration, and disillusionment. Are your friend's actions a result of unruliness, faintheartedness, weakness—or all three? Should you confront or console? Should your love be tender or tough? If you are wrestling with these issues, the following questions may help you determine a proper response.

How would you feel if you were in your friend's shoes? Would you feel trapped? Lonely? Hurt? Try to rephrase your friend's feelings without necessarily agreeing with his or her behavior.

_____

_____

_____

What needs in your friend's life are being met by worldly living? Can you see a way that Christ could satisfy them instead? How?

_____

_____

_____

With what destructive behaviors has your friend chosen to meet those needs? What will be the long-term consequences for your friend as well as those people he or she loves most?

_____

_____

_____

At this point, if you sense that your friend is determined to continue sinning in spite of the consequences, he or she is probably being unruly. How can you let this person know you care while admonishing his or her behavior?

_____

_____

_____

If he or she realizes the dangers, regrets past choices, wants to change but doesn't know how or doesn't feel strong enough, your friend needs encouragement and help. How can you strengthen and hold on to him or her as you light the way back to God?

_____

_____

_____

Finally, what hope can you give this person? Describe how you and this person can find peace and security in Christ together.

_____

_____

_____

Chapter 11

GERMS THAT MAKE US CONTAGIOUS

1 Thessalonians 5:16–22

D o you have the courage to be a contagious Christian? Perhaps you never realized that being contagious requires courage, but think about it for a moment. Releasing Christ's infectious presence in your daily life takes the courage to

- smile at life rather than dread it;

- listen to God's "You can do it!" rather than others' "Watch out!";

- be enthusiastic rather than pessimistic about what the day holds for you.

It doesn't necessarily take a dynamic personality to be contagious. For instance, we wouldn't say that Mother Teresa has a boisterous temperament, yet her vision to give love to the unlovable sick and dying has influenced untold thousands of others.

Contagious Christians inspire, challenge, and sometimes rebuke us by their example of courage. They literally "en-courage" us—put courage into our lives so we can be contagious also.

Paul understood how vital this exchange is, which is why he commanded the Thessalonian believers to "encourage one another" (1 Thess. 5:11). He longed for them to build each other up, so he gave them a list of traits that would make their faith catching. We'll review the first half of the list, which we studied in the previous chapter, and then we'll go on to the rest.

As Encouragement, Some Things Are . . .

The first things Paul lists are *kindly requested.* He asks that we respect our spiritual leaders and commit ourselves to live in peace (vv. 12–13). The next things are *urgently needed.* He urges us to admonish the unruly, put courage into the discouraged, stay with the weak, be patient with everyone, and refuse to retaliate (vv. 14–15). Let's continue now with verses 16–22.

While Others Things Are . . .

Other things Paul lists are *continually appropriate* (vv. 16–20), and one item is listed because circumstances are *occasionally uncertain* (vv. 21–22). Mix all these traits together in the lives of believers, and what do you get? Contagious Christians who spread Christ's influence wherever they go. Let's look at these appealing characteristics in more detail.

Continually Appropriate

Five qualities comprise the things that are continually appropriate. We say "continually" because Paul uses such words as *always* (v. 16), *without ceasing* (v. 17), and *in everything* (v. 18).

1. *Rejoice always* (v. 16). "Rejoicing always" doesn't require a vibrant, outgoing personality; many quiet people are contagiously joyful. Their joy is reflected in and sustained by a well-developed sense of humor, an optimistic outlook on life, a focus on the prevention and healing of problems rather than on their difficulty, and a lightness of spirit.

This kind of joyful perspective enables us to live above our circumstances and see beyond the petty differences that separate us, because at its root is the solid foundation of our faith. As one Jesuit priest wrote, "Joy is the surest sign of the presence of God."[1]

2. *Pray without ceasing* (v. 17). Paul's second command is so intertwined with the first that it's impossible to separate them. Without prayer, our joy is superficial and our smiles are painted on. Real joy emerges from a heart that's free from burdens, and the only way to be free of burdens is to release them through continual prayer.

Does that mean we have to be on our knees all day, praying for hours on end and refusing food and sleep? No. One helpful paraphrase of Paul's command is "Pray with the frequency of a hacking cough"! Have you ever had a tickle in your throat that wouldn't go away, one that made you cough all day? That's Paul's idea. Praying unceasingly means to continually send quick prayers of faith to the Lord throughout the day.

When an ornery boss makes life difficult and you feel a tickle of anxiety, release that burden in prayer. When worry or fear or impatience begin irritating you, pray a short prayer of trust in the

---

1. Pierre Teilhard de Chardin, as quoted by Bruce Larson in *There's a Lot More to Health Than Not Being Sick* (Waco, Tex.: Word Books, 1984), p. 124.

Lord. It's not a lengthy "Thou, Almighty Maker of the heavens, I beseech Thee with a contrite and lowly heart . . ." It's quicker than that. "Lord, help!" is more like it.

This kind of prayer life is tremendously therapeutic and is also an effective pipeline to God's wisdom during the day. Continual prayer helps you see your problems from God's point of view.

3. *Develop a grateful spirit* (v. 18). As a result of ceaseless prayer, we nurture not only a joyful heart but a grateful spirit as well, which Paul highlights next.

> In everything give thanks; for this is God's will for you in Christ Jesus. (v. 18)

Paul doesn't say we are to be grateful *for* everything, but *in* everything. There's a significant distinction. We aren't thankful for our sinful behaviors or the consequences they bring, nor do we say, "Thank you, Lord, that someone hurt my child's feelings today." We don't have to thank the Lord for the storms of life, but we can be grateful that, through the rain and thunder, God is producing within us a spiritual harvest.

4. *Do not quench the Spirit* (v. 19). Having listed three positive traits, Paul now switches to the negative.[2] We could paraphrase this as, "Stop putting out the Spirit's fire!"

We know that the Holy Spirit won't leave us because the Lord has promised Him to us as a powerful guiding force and a seal of our redemption (see John 14:16–17; Eph. 1:13–14). He is a fire within us that burns away sin and softens our hearts to God. He sensitizes us to spiritual things and the hurting cries of those around us, then heats up our passion to tell the world about Christ. However, we can choose not to listen to His voice, smothering His influence with a blanket of stubbornness or pride. He is still there, ready to ignite our hearts again, but He won't force Himself on us. His influence smoldering, He simply steps back, folds His arms, and waits.

The prophet Hosea observed God dealing with the sinful people of Israel (here called Ephraim) in this same way. At first, He tried chastising them to bring them back to Himself (Hos. 5:2–3). They

---

2. In Paul's first three commands, the Greek structure emphasized the adverbs: "*always* rejoice," "*unceasingly* pray," "*in everything* give thanks." In these next two commands, his phrasing highlights the nouns: "the *Spirit,* do not extinguish," "*prophetic utterances* do not despise."

did not repent but were "determined to follow man's command" (v. 11b). Hosea records what the Lord did next in God's own words:

> Therefore I am like a moth to Ephraim,
> And like rottenness to the house of Judah. (v. 12)

To get their attention, He became a fluttering, tormenting moth in their eyes. But they waved Him off and went to Assyria for help instead (v. 13). What did the Lord do next?

> For I will be like a lion to Ephraim,
> And like a young lion to the house of Judah.
> I, even I, will tear to pieces and go away,
> I will carry away, and there will be none to
>   deliver. (v. 14)

From a pesky moth to a growling, clawing lion, the Lord was going to extremes to restore Israel's faith. Still they did not repent! So, the Lord says,

> I will go away and return to My place
> Until they acknowledge their guilt and seek My
>   face;
> In their affliction they will earnestly seek Me.
> (v. 15)

Divine silence, the affliction of God's absence, the worst imaginable discipline for a believer. Better for God to be a roaring lion than a wisp of air, leaving a tomb-like hush and a cold, barren loneliness.

As a result of their sin, the people had to bear the consequences:

> Ephraim is joined to idols;
> Let him alone. (4:17)

When we walk away from the Spirit, He lets us alone too. Obstinately pursuing our own idols, we keep pushing Him away until finally He says, "OK, you're on your own." But if we fan the flames and remain dependent and obedient, we'll once again experience His active power within our lives—a contagious presence of God for all to see.

5. *Do not despise prophetic utterances* (1 Thess. 5:20). Apparently, the Thessalonian believers were discounting all prophecy in their church because of a few false prophets—perhaps the very ones who had quit their jobs and were spreading wrong information about future events. The Apostle advises the people, "Do not despise

prophetic utterances," because they still needed to listen to the genuine prophets who spoke God's Word.

We, too, need to hear and obey God's Word as revealed in the Old and New Testaments. And we need to take seriously the wise counsel given by those whom God uses to speak to us.[3]

Occasionally Uncertain

Finally, because some things are occasionally uncertain, we must "examine everything carefully" (v. 21a). "Be discerning," Paul is saying; "Put everything to the test." Here's a threefold test we can use to determine what is and isn't of God:

1. Is it consistent with the truth of Scripture?

2. Is it obedient to the lordship of Christ?

3. Is it in agreement with my inner spirit?

Then, having examined everything carefully, "hold fast to that which is good; abstain from every form of evil" (vv. 21b–22).

Therefore, If You Hope to Encourage Others . . .

Do you have the courage to be a contagious Christian? We've listed the traits required—are you ready to accept them as your own? If so, keep in mind the following three Rs: *Remember*, the goal is to be an encouragement to others (v. 11). *Resist* the cheap imitations of spirituality, such as superficial laughter instead of joy, or automatic prayers instead of unceasing prayer. *Release* your fear of what others might say or think. Don't just play the game on Sundays but become too afraid to live for Christ during the week. Don't settle for mediocrity in your Christian life because you might ruffle some feathers. Instead, be confident in the faith God has given you. Have courage!

---

3. Technically, a prophet was someone who spoke without error the revealed oracles of God. Because we have the completed Word of God, these types of prophets are no longer needed. Generally speaking, prophecy can be "the declaration of God's mind spoken forthrightly in the power of the Spirit at just the right time." These words come as wise exhortations from people who challenge us to live according to God's Word.

Having listed the "germs" that make your Christianity contagious, we remind you of one remaining ingredient: time. Changes in attitude occur slowly as you incorporate these traits into your life. So, as you reflect on these traits, consider how you can practice them not just today, but in the many days ahead.

Rejoice always. Since prayerful trust produces richer joy, in what areas do you need to trust the Lord? If worry has been affecting your countenance, how can you change your grim frown into a relaxed smile?

_____

_____

_____

Pray without ceasing. What burdens do you need to release to the Lord? How can you remind yourself to keep releasing your burdens throughout the day?

_____

_____

Develop a grateful spirit. Have you been taking for granted the Lord's gifts to you? In what ways can you express your gratitude more regularly? What are some difficult circumstances in your life right now in which you can be thankful?

_____

_____

Do not quench the Spirit. Have you sensed the Spirit igniting your heart with a passion for spiritual things? If not, in what ways might you be quenching His fire? How can you fuel His flame instead?

_____

Do not despise prophetic utterances. Lately, have you sloughed off the wise counsel from Scripture that someone gave you?

Examine everything carefully. Have friends been offering you worldly counsel lately? If so, examine it carefully, and determine to "hold fast to that which is good" and "abstain from every form of evil" (1 Thess. 5:21b–22).

Living Insights

In Spain, a symbol of courage is the matador. Armed only with a red cape and a sword that looks like a long knitting needle, he enters the arena on foot to battle an unpredictable, hot-tempered bull. With each pass of the beast, the matador deftly steps to the side and swings his cape in a graceful arch. One slip, one lapse in his concentration could mean serious injury and even death. Where is the school that teaches a matador the courage to face hundreds of raging bulls during his career? One of Spain's most successful matadors, El Cordobés, answered that question simply: "The university for courage is to do what you believe in!"[4]

The same advice applies to Christians who must enter the world's arena every day. Courage comes by doing what we believe in. Are you facing a fearsome problem that is ready to charge you

---

4. El Cordobés (Manuel Benitez Perez), as quoted in *Simpson's Contemporary Quotations,* comp. James B. Simpson (Boston, Mass.: Houghton Mifflin Co., 1988), p. 385.

at any moment? What is the situation? How courageous are you feeling now?

_____

_____

_____

In what ways can obeying Paul's commands give you needed courage?

_____

_____

_____

What will you do today to stand tall and face your difficulty in the arena?

_____

_____

_____

Chapter 12

WHAT A WAY TO SAY GOOD-BYE!

1 Thessalonians 5:23–28

The ticket is in hand and the flight attendant has made the final boarding call. The dreaded moment is here . . . it is time to say good-bye.

A son or daughter may be going to college. A visiting sweetheart may be returning home. A grandparent may be moving away. We've all experienced these kinds of good-byes. First, there is small talk: "Looks like good weather for the trip." "Write soon." "I promise." Then one last embrace. And tears. "You're gonna miss your flight." "I love you." Tears. The walk through the tunnel. Then a final turn and wave: "Good-bye."

How we dislike saying good-bye. We don't even like the word! We'd rather say, "See ya later" or "Keep in touch" or "Talk to you soon." *Good-bye* can be so final. But, as wrenching as it is, saying good-bye can be an opportunity to turn our attention to the Lord and focus on the security He provides. If said well, a good-bye can ignite a hopeful flame of God's presence in the hearts of the ones leaving and in those staying behind.

Paul concludes his letter to the Thessalonians with such a fare-well. Instead of ending with a breezy, "Keep smilin'! Yours truly, Paul," he takes six verses to graciously affirm his readers with a benediction that is the emotional capstone of his entire letter.

A Brief Review: The Letter as a Whole

From the start, Paul has constantly expressed his affection to-ward his readers. Since these people were among his first converts in Europe, he must have felt a unique oneness with them such as a mother senses toward her firstborn child. Each chapter of 1 Thessalonians has him saying something special to these believers:

Chapter 1—"I give thanks for you" (vv. 1–2)
Chapter 2—"I love you dearly" (vv. 7–8)
Chapter 3—"I am concerned about you" (vv. 4–5)
Chapter 4—"I exhort you" (vv. 1–3, 9–11)
Chapter 5—"I encourage you" (vv. 11–14)

Having poured out his heart in so many ways, it must have been difficult to now say good-bye. Yet, tenderly, he writes his farewell in a way that brings their hearts closer to God's.

A Profound Farewell: The Writer as a Friend

Three aspects comprise Paul's benediction: first, his thoughts about the Lord (5:23–24); second, his words to the people (vv. 25–27); and finally, his favorite theme, grace (v. 28).

God, Who Is Faithful

Paul's good-bye is actually a prayer and a blessing at the same time. F. F. Bruce calls it a "wish-prayer,"[1] because instead of saying, "Father, may You do this for these people," he prays, "May God do this for you." In a sense, Paul is praying with his eyes open and looking directly at his dear friends.

His prayer begins: "Now may the God of peace Himself sanctify you entirely" (v. 23a). For the last two chapters, he has been pointing his finger at his readers, challenging them to live in sexual purity (4:1–8) and warning them about behaving properly toward outsiders (vv. 9–12). He has been addressing their misconceptions about the Lord's coming (4:13–5:11) and listing about a dozen top-priority commands for them to follow (5:12–22). Now, in his conclusion, he points to the only One who can help them obey these instructions—the faithful God.

And he does this quite emphatically. In the original Greek, *Himself* appears as the first word in the sentence, underscoring God's personal involvement and pointing to His name: the "God of peace." This is an ancient title. It first appeared with the Hebrew word *shalom*, which means "wholeness" (see Judg. 6:24). The Greek word used here, *eirēnē*, also suggests "harmony, friendliness, and contentment." Our Lord, then, is a God of:

- harmony, not disorder, chaos or confusion

- friendliness, not irritability, anxiety, or impatience

- contentment, not restlessness, impulsiveness, or hurry

---

1. F. F. Bruce, *1 and 2 Thessalonians*, Word Biblical Commentary series, vol. 45 (Waco, Tex.: Word Books, 1982), p. 129.

How unlike our God of peace are idols of stone! Their eyes glare at you; their mouths twist into merciless grimaces; smoke billows out of their nostrils. They are demanding gods, easily offended and never satisfied.

But our God has compassion filling His eyes because His wrath has been appeased at the Cross. We don't have to drag our good deeds before Him like sacrificial offerings, hoping He's in a good mood that day. He demands nothing more of us for salvation than that we receive His love and forgiveness as a gift. Christ's blood has done the work of atonement, and God is satisfied.

As a result, according to Paul's wish-prayer, God is able to do three things for us—first, sanctify us entirely; second, preserve us completely; and third, receive us blamelessly.

May He set you apart entirely. Paul prays that God may "sanctify you entirely" (1 Thess. 5:23), reflecting his desire that God set apart the Thessalonians from evil. While the root meaning of sanctification is to be made holy or separate from sin, this does not imply that we have to cloister ourselves in a monastery. Nor does it mean we have to dress in plain-wrap clothes, suppress our natural personalities, and wear somber expressions so as not to appear worldly. Sanctification has nothing to do with temperament or external religious trappings. It is God removing, little by little, the poison of sin that contaminates us, freeing us to become who He created us to be.

May He preserve you completely. The Apostle next prays, "May your spirit and soul and body be preserved complete" (v. 23b). The Greek word for *preserve* is *tēreō*, which means "to watch over, guard, keep."[2] From what does he ask God to keep us? The contamination of the sinful world. Think of a cook who preserves fruits and vegetables in sterile, tightly sealed jars—God seals us with His Spirit to keep the mold of sin from growing on our hearts. To do so, He doesn't remove us from the world, but insulates us within it. Remember Jesus' prayer?

> "I do not ask Thee to take them out of the world,
> but to keep them from the evil one." (John 17:15)

---

2. G. Abbott-Smith, *A Manual Greek Lexicon of the New Testament,* 3d ed. (Edinburgh, Scotland: T. and T. Clark, 1937), p. 445.

"Preserved complete" is Paul's way of praying the same thing, adding the request that God watch over not just our external actions but our whole person: "spirit and soul and body."[3]

May He receive you blameless. The goal of God's sanctifying and preserving is that we be "without blame at the coming of our Lord Jesus Christ" (1 Thess. 5:23c). Imagine the joy of standing before the Lord without fault, with no rebuke, no condemnation, no guilt—all because of the Cross. What freedom and confidence that brings! Jude's benediction in his letter contains the same wonderful thought:

> Now to Him who is able to keep you from stumbling, and to make you stand in the presence of His glory blameless with great joy, to the only God our Savior, through Jesus Christ our Lord, be glory, majesty, dominion and authority, before all time and now and forever. Amen. (vv. 24–25)

In Christ, we have all we need—forgiveness, hope, and freedom from guilt. If we ever have doubts concerning our salvation, Paul reminds us:

> Faithful is He who calls you, and He also will bring it to pass. (1 Thess. 5:24)

God does it all! Our old sinful heart condemns us, but He has given us a new heart. In a way, our experience is similar to Philip Blaiberg's. One of Dr. Christiaan Barnard's first heart-transplant patients, he was asked by the famous surgeon if he would like to see his old heart. Blaiberg said yes, and the doctor handed him a glass container.

> A few moments of silence followed as for the first time in history a man actually gazed at his own heart. Then the two men talked about it. Finally Philip Blaiberg said, "So that is the old heart that caused

---

3. Phrases like this have kept theologians speculating for centuries about what our person is comprised of. The trichotomist view of our personhood, as explained by Charles C. Ryrie, states that we have three aspects: "Body relates to self, soul to the world, but spirit to God." The dichotomist perspective is: "Man is made up of two substances, material and immaterial. Each consists of a variety within. The many facets of the material and the many facets of the immaterial join together to make up the whole of each person." *Basic Theology* (Wheaton, Ill.: Scripture Press Publications, Victor Books, 1986), p. 196.

me so much trouble," and he handed it back, turned away, and left it forever.[4]

We see the trouble our old hearts cause us, and we're so grateful that the Lord has given us a new chance at life. He's signed us, sealed us, and at Christ's coming, will Himself deliver us blameless to heaven.

Friends, Who Are Loyal

Having focused on the Lord, Paul now draws the reader's attention to relationships within the body. He states three things loyal friends do for one another.

First, *they pray for each other*. "Brethren, pray for us," Paul writes (v. 25), reminding us that prayer is a serious responsibility between close friends. If the Apostle, who was spiritually mature, needed others to pray for him, how much more do we need our brothers and sisters to pray for us—and how much they need us to pray for them. Intercession is one of the surest signs of your sincere loyalty and love.

Second, *they affirm and show affection for each other*. Paul also says, "Greet all the brethren with a holy kiss" (v. 26). This kiss of greeting symbolized an acceptance of all believers, regardless of status or race. Commentator W. E. Vine explains:

> There was to be an absence of formality and hypocrisy, a freedom from prejudice arising from social distinctions, from discrimination against the poor, from partiality towards the well-to-do. In the churches masters and servants would thus salute one another without any attitude of condescension on the one part or disrespect on the other. The kiss took place thus between persons of the same sex.[5]

In our culture, greeting one another with a hug or a kiss sometimes symbolizes that same kind of acceptance and is an appropriate expression of affection. At other times, such a gesture just makes people feel uncomfortable. The point Paul is making is that we are

4. As told by Ian Barclay in *Living and Enjoying the Fruit of the Spirit* (Chicago, Ill.: Moody Press, 1975), p. 55.

5. W. E. Vine, *Vine's Expository Dictionary of Old and New Testament Words* (Old Tappan, N.J.: Fleming H. Revell Co., 1981), vol. 2, p. 296.

to show one another that we care about them, whether by a kiss on the cheek, a hug, a warm handshake, or a pat on the shoulder—the method isn't as important as the message of love.

Finally, *loyal friends listen to the same information*. In a firm tone, Paul commands the Thessalonians:

> I adjure you by the Lord to have this letter read to all the brethren. (v. 27)

This statement has the weight of an oath before God. Perhaps splinter groups were beginning to form in the church, and Paul wanted them to listen to his words from the Lord together. Whatever the reason, they were to keep each other accountable to the commands in this letter. In our churches, we can heed Paul's words by encouraging one another to turn to the Word, working together to increase our love for and obedience to His message.

Grace, Which Is Lasting

As Paul began his letter, "Grace to you and peace" (1:1b), so he ends it, "The grace of our Lord Jesus Christ be with you" (5:28).

The word *grace* has many nuances that sparkle like facets of a diamond.[6] It includes the ideas of favor, beauty, thanksgiving, delight, kindness, and benefit—even charm and joy. Essentially, it refers to that which produces well-being. It is always something undeserved, immeasurable, overflowing, freely given, and impossible to repay. Theologically speaking, grace is God's favor that is lovingly, lavishly, endlessly bestowed upon us because of Christ. All this radiates from Paul's simple yet eloquent farewell. What a way to say good-bye!

A Final Thought: The Truth as a Guide

Aren't you glad you've become friends with this encouraging book of the Bible? It's challenged you to increase your faith, to rest more in the hope of Christ's coming, and to genuinely love your brothers and sisters in Christ. Faith, hope, and love—Paul's gifts to his newborn church in Thessalonica and the three points of light in the night sky that can guide us to becoming more like Christ.

---

6. The Greek word for *grace* is *charis*, which means "kindness, goodwill, favour." The verb *charizomai* means "to show favour or kindness . . . to give freely." And the noun *charisma* means "a free gift." See Abbott-Smith, *Manual Greek Lexicon*, pp. 479–80.

We conclude our study with the same good-bye to you that Paul wrote to his beloved friends. Eugene Peterson's version of the New Testament, *The Message*, serves as our translation:

> *May God himself, the God who makes everything holy and whole, make you holy and whole, put you together—spirit, soul, and body—and keep you fit for the coming of our Master, Jesus Christ. The One who called you is completely dependable. If he said it, he'll do it!*
>
> *Friends, keep up your prayers for us. Greet all the Christians there with a holy embrace. And make sure this letter gets read to all the brothers and sisters. Don't leave anyone out.*
>
> *The amazing grace of Jesus Christ be with you!* [7]

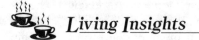

Living Insights

Are you going to have to say good-bye to someone dear to you? Perhaps a good friend is moving out of state or a visiting relative you don't see very often is going home soon. How can you say good-bye in a way that will leave a flame of God's presence glowing in that person's heart? Use Paul's outline to formulate your own farewell blessing.

First, focus on the Lord. What do you pray that the Lord will do for your friend or relative? Review 1 Thessalonians 3:11–13 as well as 5:23–24.

_____

_____

_____

Next, consider your relationship with this person. What promises can you make that will assure him or her that you are a loyal friend? See verses 25–27.

_____

7. Eugene H. Peterson, *The Message: The New Testament in Contemporary English* (Colorado Springs, Colo.: NavPress, 1993), p. 434.

Finally, leave them with grace. What facet of God's gemlike grace do you wish for them to experience? See verse 28.

_____

_____

_____

☕ *Living Insights* STUDY TWO

To fully enjoy a cup of coffee, it needs to be savored. In the same way, we ask you to take a few moments to review 1 Thessalonians from beginning to end. Page through the preceding chapters of this study guide and freshen your memory concerning the main themes. Scan the five chapters of the book in your Bible as well, and mark the verses that spoke to you personally. Then, in the following space, write down the principles and lessons from each chapter of Paul's letter that mean the most to you. This can be the most satisfying part of your Bible study. Savor it slowly!

Chapter 1 _____

_____

_____

Chapter 2 _____

_____

_____

Chapter 3 _____

_____

_____

Chapter 4 _____

Chapter 5

In light of these principles, what changes in your life can you start making today?

BOOKS FOR PROBING FURTHER

You've probably seen an epilogue scrolling up the screen at the end of a movie, giving follow-up information about the main characters. In a way, Paul provided such an epilogue to his Thessalonian letters in 2 Corinthians, where he held up the Macedonian churches—including the church in Thessalonica—as models of Christian love and charity (see 8:1–5). Based on what Paul wrote, our Thessalonian epilogue might read:

> *Despite continued affliction and deep poverty, the*
> *Thessalonians remain firm in their faith, vibrant in hope,*
> *and overflowing in generous love.*

That's contagious Christianity! Our prayer is that as a result of your study of 1 Thessalonians, someone will write a similar epilogue about your life. We've provided the following resources to help you further apply principles for contagious living.

Commentaries on 1 Thessalonians

Morris, Leon. *The First and Second Epistles to the Thessalonians.* Rev. ed. The New International Commentary on the New Testament series. Grand Rapids, Mich.: William B. Eerdmans Publishing Co., 1991.

Stott, John R. *The Gospel and the End of Time: The Message of 1 and 2 Thessalonians.* Downers Grove, Ill.: InterVarsity Press, 1991.

Toward Contagious Joy

McCullough, Donald W. *Finding Happiness in the Most Unlikely Places.* Downers Grove, Ill.: InterVarsity Press, 1990.

Swindoll, Charles R. *Laugh Again: Experience Outrageous Joy.* Dallas, Tex.: Word Publishing, 1992.

Toward Contagious Relationships

McDowell, Josh. *The Secret of Loving.* San Bernardino, Calif.: Here's Life Publishers, 1985.

Petersen, Jim. *Living Proof.* Colorado Springs, Colo.: NavPress, 1989.

Wright, H. Norman. *How to Get Along with Almost Anyone.* Dallas, Tex.: Word Publishing, 1989.

Toward Contagious Moral Purity

Durfield, Richard C., and Reneé Durfield. *Raising Them Chaste.* Minneapolis, Minn.: Bethany House Publishers, 1991.

Stafford, Tim. *A Love Story: Questions and Answers on Sex.* Wheaton, Ill.: Tyndale House Publishers, Campus Life Books, 1987.

———. *Sexual Chaos.* Rev. ed. Downers Grove, Ill.: InterVarsity Press, 1993.

Toward Contagious Faith

Lucado, Max. *He Still Moves Stones.* Dallas, Tex.: Word Publishing, 1993.

Sproul, R. C. *Surprised by Suffering.* Wheaton, Ill.: Tyndale House Publishers, 1988.

Tada, Joni Eareckson. *Seeking God: My Journey of Prayer and Praise.* Brentwood, Tenn.: Wolgemuth and Hyatt, Publishers, 1991.

Toward Contagious Leadership

Covey, Stephen R. *Principle-Centered Leadership.* New York, N.Y.: Simon and Schuster, Summit Books, 1991.

Ford, Leighton. *Transforming Leadership: Jesus' Way of Creating Vision, Shaping Values and Empowering Change.* Downers Grove, Ill.: InterVarsity Press, 1991.

Smith, Fred. *Learning to Lead: Bringing Out the Best in People.* Carol Stream, Ill.: Christianity Today; Waco, Tex.: Word Books, 1986.

All of the books listed above are recommended reading; however, some may be out of print and available only through a library. For books currently available, please contact your local Christian bookstore. Works by Charles R. Swindoll are available through Insight for Living. IFL also offers some books by other authors— please note the Ordering Information that follows and contact the office which serves you.

ORDERING INFORMATION

CONTAGIOUS CHRISTIANITY

Cassette Tapes and Study Guide

This Bible study guide was designed to be used independently or in conjunction with the broadcast of Chuck Swindoll's taped messages on the topic listed below. If you would like to order cassette tapes or further copies of this study guide, please see the information given below and the Order Form provided at the end of this guide.

		U.S.	Canada
CCH SG	Study guide	$ 3.95	$ 5.25
CCH CS	Cassette series,	42.55	51.25
	includes album cover		
CCH 1–6	Individual cassettes,	6.30	8.00
	includes messages A and B		

The prices are subject to change without notice.

CCH 1-A: *A Church with the Right Stuff*—1 Thessalonians 1
B: *A Leadership Style That Works . . . Guaranteed!*—
1 Thessalonians 2:1–12

CCH 2-A: *The Flip Side of Leadership*—1 Thessalonians 2:13–20
B: *When Your Comfort Zone Gets the Squeeze*—
1 Thessalonians 3:1–8

CCH 3-A: *What Does It Mean to "Really Live"?*—
1 Thessalonians 3:9–13
B: *Straight Talk about Moral Purity*—1 Thessalonians 4:1–8

CCH 4-A: *Behaving Properly toward Outsiders*—
1 Thessalonians 4:9–12
B: *On That Great Gettin'-Up Morning*—
1 Thessalonians 4:13–18

CCH 5-A: *". . . Like a Thief in the Night"*—1 Thessalonians 5:1–11
B: *Gifts to Give the Family*—1 Thessalonians 5:12–15

CCH 6-A: *Germs That Make Us Contagious*—
1 Thessalonians 5:16–22
B: *What a Way to Say Good-bye!*—1 Thessalonians 5:23–28

How to Order by Phone or FAX
(Credit card orders only)

United States: 1-800-772-8888 from 7:00 A.M. to 4:30 P.M., Pacific time, Monday through Friday
FAX (714) 575-5496 anytime, day or night

Canada: 1-800-663-7639, Vancouver residents call (604) 596-2910 from 7:00 A.M. to 5:00 P.M., Pacific time, Monday through Friday
FAX (604) 596-2975 anytime, day or night

Australia: (03) 872-4606 or FAX (03) 874-8890 from 9:00 A.M. to 5:00 P.M., Monday through Friday

---

Other International Locations: call the Ordering Services Department in the United States at (714) 575-5000 during the hours listed above.

How to Order by Mail

United States
- Mail to: Ordering Services Department
  Insight for Living
  Post Office Box 69000
  Anaheim, CA 92817-0900
- Sales tax: California residents add 7.25%.
- Shipping: add 10% of the total order amount for first-class delivery. (Otherwise, allow four to six weeks for fourth-class delivery.)
- Payment: personal checks, money orders, credit cards (Visa, MasterCard, Discover Card). No invoices or COD orders available.
- $10 fee for *any* returned check.

Canada
- Mail to: Insight for Living Ministries
  Post Office Box 2510
  Vancouver, BC V6B 3W7
- Sales tax: Please add 7% GST. British Columbia residents also add 7% sales tax (on tapes or cassette series).
- Shipping: included in prices listed above.
- Payment: personal checks, money orders, credit cards (Visa, Master-Card). No invoices or COD orders available.

- Delivery: approximately four weeks.

Australia, New Zealand, or Papua New Guinea
- Mail to: Insight for Living, Inc.
  GPO Box 2823 EE
  Melbourne, Victoria 3001, Australia
- Shipping and delivery time: please see chart that follows.
- Payment: personal checks payable in U.S. funds, international money orders, or credit cards (Visa, MasterCard).

Other International Locations
- Mail to: Ordering Services Department
  Insight for Living
  Post Office Box 69000
  Anaheim, CA 92817-0900
- Shipping and delivery time: please see chart that follows.
- Payment: personal checks payable in U.S. funds, international money orders, or credit cards (Visa, MasterCard).

Type of Shipping	Postage Cost	Delivery
Surface	10% of total order*	6 to 10 weeks
Airmail	25% of total order*	under 6 weeks

*Use U.S. price as a base.

Our Guarantee

Your complete satisfaction is our top priority here at Insight for Living. If you're not completely satisfied with anything you order, please return it for full credit, a refund, or a replacement, as you prefer.

Insight for Living Catalog

The Insight for Living catalog features study guides, tapes, and books by a variety of Christian authors. To obtain a free copy, call us at the numbers listed above.

Order Form
United States, Australia, and Overseas
(Canadian residents please use Order Form on reverse side.)

CCH CS represents the entire *Contagious Christianity* series in a special album cover, while CCH 1–6 are the individual tapes included in the series. CCH SG represents this study guide, should you desire to order additional copies.

CCH	SG	Study guide	$ 3.95
CCH	CS	Cassette series,	42.55
		includes album cover	
CCH	1–6	Individual cassettes,	6.30
		includes messages A and B	

Product Code	Product Description	Quantity	Unit Price	Total
			$	$
	Subtotal			
	California Residents—Sales Tax *Add 7.25% of subtotal.*			
	U.S. First-Class Shipping *For faster delivery, add 10% for postage and handling.*			
	Non-United States Residents *U.S. price plus 10% surface postage or 25% airmail.*			
	Gift to Insight for Living *Tax-deductible in the United States.*			
	Total Amount Due *Please do not send cash.*		$	

Prices are subject to change without notice.

Payment by: ❑ Check or money order payable to Insight for Living   ❑ Credit card

(Circle one): Visa   MasterCard   Discover Card   Number _____

Expiration Date _____   Signature _____
We cannot process your credit card purchase without your signature.

Name _____

Address _____

City _____   State _____

Zip Code _____   Country _____

Telephone (___) _____   Radio Station ___ ___ ___ ___
If questions arise concerning your order, we may need to contact you.

Mail this order form to the Ordering Services Department at one of these addresses:

Insight for Living
Post Office Box 69000, Anaheim, CA 92817-0900

Insight for Living, Inc.
GPO Box 2823 EE, Melbourne, VIC 3001, Australia

Order Form
Canadian Residents

(Residents of the United States, Australia, and other international locations,
please use Order Form on reverse side.)

CCH CS represents the entire *Contagious Christianity* series in a special album cover, while
CCH 1–6 are the individual tapes included in the series. CCH SG represents this study
guide, should you desire to order additional copies.

CCH	SG	Study guide	$ 5.25
CCH	CS	Cassette series,	51.25
		includes album cover	
CCH	1–6	Individual cassettes,	8.00
		includes messages A and B	

Product Code	Product Description	Quantity	Unit Price	Total
			$	$
		Subtotal		
		Add 7% GST		
	British Columbia Residents *Add 7% sales tax on individual tapes or cassette series.*			
	Gift to Insight for Living Ministries *Tax-deductible in Canada.*			
	Total Amount Due *Please do not send cash.*		$	

Prices are subject to change without notice.

Payment by: ❑ Check or money order payable to Insight for Living Ministries
❑ Credit card

(Circle one): Visa   MasterCard   Number _____

Expiration Date _____   Signature _____

We cannot process your credit card purchase without your signature.

Name _____

Address _____

City _____ Province _____

Postal Code _____ . Country _____

Telephone ( ) _____ Radio Station ____ ____ ____ ____
If questions arise concerning your order, we may need to contact you.

Mail this order form to the Ordering Services Department at the following address:

Insight for Living Ministries
Post Office Box 2510
Vancouver, BC, Canada V6B 3W7

Order Form
United States, Australia, and Overseas
(Canadian residents please use Order Form on reverse side.)

CCH CS represents the entire *Contagious Christianity* series in a special album cover, while CCH 1–6 are the individual tapes included in the series. CCH SG represents this study guide, should you desire to order additional copies.

CCH	SG	Study guide	$ 3.95
CCH	CS	Cassette series,	42.55
		includes album cover	
CCH	1–6	Individual cassettes,	6.30
		includes messages A and B	

Product Code	Product Description	Quantity	Unit Price	Total
			$	$
		Subtotal		
		California Residents—Sales Tax *Add 7.25% of subtotal.*		
		U.S. First-Class Shipping *For faster delivery, add 10% for postage and handling.*		
		Non-United States Residents *U.S. price plus 10% surface postage or 25% airmail.*		
		Gift to Insight for Living *Tax-deductible in the United States.*		
		Total Amount Due *Please do not send cash.*	$	

Prices are subject to change without notice.

Payment by: ❏ Check or money order payable to Insight for Living   ❏ Credit card

(Circle one): Visa   MasterCard   Discover Card   Number _____

Expiration Date_____   Signature_____
We cannot process your credit card purchase without your signature.

Name_____

Address_____

City_____   State_____

Zip Code_____   Country_____

Telephone (_____)_____   Radio Station____ ____ ____ ____
If questions arise concerning your order, we may need to contact you.

Mail this order form to the Ordering Services Department at one of these addresses:

> **Insight for Living**
> Post Office Box 69000, Anaheim, CA 92817-0900
>
> **Insight for Living, Inc.**
> GPO Box 2823 EE, Melbourne, VIC 3001, Australia

Order Form
Canadian Residents

(Residents of the United States, Australia, and other international locations, please use Order Form on reverse side.)

CCH CS represents the entire *Contagious Christianity* series in a special album cover, while CCH 1–6 are the individual tapes included in the series. CCH SG represents this study guide, should you desire to order additional copies.

CCH	SG	Study guide	$ 5.25
CCH	CS	Cassette series, includes album cover	51.25
CCH	1–6	Individual cassettes, includes messages A and B	8.00

Product Code	Product Description	Quantity	Unit Price	Total
			$	$

Subtotal	
Add 7% GST	
British Columbia Residents *Add 7% sales tax on individual tapes or cassette series.*	
Gift to Insight for Living Ministries *Tax-deductible in Canada.*	
Total Amount Due *Please do not send cash.*	$

Prices are subject to change without notice.

Payment by: ❏ Check or money order payable to Insight for Living Ministries
❏ Credit card

(Circle one): Visa   MasterCard   Number _____

Expiration Date _____   Signature _____
We cannot process your credit card purchase without your signature.

Name _____

Address _____

City _____ Province _____

Postal Code _____ Country _____

Telephone (___) _____ Radio Station ___ ___ ___ ___
If questions arise concerning your order, we may need to contact you.

Mail this order form to the Ordering Services Department at the following address:

Insight for Living Ministries
Post Office Box 2510
Vancouver, BC, Canada V6B 3W7

Order Form
United States, Australia, and Overseas
(Canadian residents please use Order Form on reverse side.)

CCH CS represents the entire *Contagious Christianity* series in a special album cover, while CCH 1–6 are the individual tapes included in the series. CCH SG represents this study guide, should you desire to order additional copies.

CCH	SG	Study guide	$ 3.95
CCH	CS	Cassette series, includes album cover	42.55
CCH	1–6	Individual cassettes, includes messages A and B	6.30

Product Code	Product Description	Quantity	Unit Price	Total
			$	$
		Subtotal		
		California Residents—Sales Tax *Add 7.25% of subtotal.*		
		U.S. First-Class Shipping *For faster delivery, add 10% for postage and handling.*		
		Non-United States Residents *U.S. price plus 10% surface postage or 25% airmail.*		
		Gift to Insight for Living *Tax-deductible in the United States.*		
		Total Amount Due *Please do not send cash.*	$	

Prices are subject to change without notice.

Payment by: ❑ Check or money order payable to Insight for Living ❑ Credit card

(Circle one): Visa MasterCard Discover Card Number _____

Expiration Date _____ Signature _____
We cannot process your credit card purchase without your signature.

Name _____

Address _____

City _____ State _____

Zip Code _____ Country _____

Telephone (___) _____ Radio Station ____ ____ ____ ____
If questions arise concerning your order, we may need to contact you.

Mail this order form to the Ordering Services Department at one of these addresses:

Insight for Living
Post Office Box 69000, Anaheim, CA 92817-0900

Insight for Living, Inc.
GPO Box 2823 EE, Melbourne, VIC 3001, Australia

Order Form
Canadian Residents
(Residents of the United States, Australia, and other international locations,
please use Order Form on reverse side.)

CCH CS represents the entire *Contagious Christianity* series in a special album cover, while CCH 1–6 are the individual tapes included in the series. CCH SG represents this study guide, should you desire to order additional copies.

CCH	SG	Study guide	$ 5.25
CCH	CS	Cassette series, includes album cover	51.25
CCH	1–6	Individual cassettes, includes messages A and B	8.00

Product Code	Product Description	Quantity	Unit Price	Total
			$	$
		Subtotal		
		Add 7% GST		
		British Columbia Residents Add 7% sales tax on individual tapes or cassette series.		
		Gift to Insight for Living Ministries Tax-deductible in Canada.		
		Total Amount Due Please do not send cash.	$	

Prices are subject to change without notice.

Payment by: ❑ Check or money order payable to Insight for Living Ministries
❑ Credit card

(Circle one): Visa   MasterCard   Number_____

Expiration Date_____   Signature_____
We cannot process your credit card purchase without your signature.

Name_____

Address_____

City_____   Province_____

Postal Code_____   Country_____

Telephone (_____)_____   Radio Station____ ____ ____ ____
If questions arise concerning your order, we may need to contact you.

Mail this order form to the Ordering Services Department at the following address:

Insight for Living Ministries
Post Office Box 2510
Vancouver, BC, Canada V6B 3W7